1 BUSINESS, 2 APPROACHES:
HOW TO SUCCEED IN INTERNET BUSINESS BY EMPLOYING REAL-WORLD STRATEGIES

1 BUSINESS, 2 APPROACHES:
HOW TO SUCCEED IN INTERNET BUSINESS BY EMPLOYING REAL-WORLD STRATEGIES

Ron E. Gielgun

 Actium Publishing, Brooklyn, New York

Editor: Robin Quinn

Printed in the United Stated of America.

2 3 4 5 6 7 8 9 10   99   00   01   02   03

Publisher's Cataloging-in-Publication
(provided by Quality Books, Inc.)

Gielgun, Ron E.
    1 business, 2 approaches: how to succeed in Internet business by employing real-world strategies/Ron E. Gielgun. — 1st ed.
    p. cm.
    Includes index.
    ISBN 0-9657617-6-2

    1. Internet marketing 2. Internet advertising 3. Internet (Computer network) 4. Business communication 5. Business enterprises--Computer networks.
    I. Title   II. Title: One business, two approaches

HF5415.1265.G54 1998   658.8'00285'4678
                            QBI98-815

Library of Congress Catalog Card Number: 98-71760

Table of Contents

Chapter 7
ADVERTISING AND MAIL ORDER 135

PREFACE

A basic premise of this book is that the Internet should be viewed as a new way to reach existing markets rather than as a new market onto itself. Successful Internet entrepreneurs take into account the real world, with its market systems and opportunities. Most important of all, they realize that not all consumers have access to the Internet. The next generation of online businesses will not be "pure" Internet businesses. Rather, they will resemble a floating iceberg, with most of the body "sunk" in the real word, and only the tip protruding into the online world for its users to see. This book will show you how to combine the best of both worlds to achieve financial success.

Ron E. Gielgun

Disclaimer

This book is sold with the understanding that the publisher and author are not engaged in rendering legal, accounting or other professional services. It is designed to provide information about the subject matter covered. It is not the purpose of this book to reprint all the information that is otherwise available to the author and/or publisher. The text in this book should be used only as a general guide and not as the ultimate source of information for the subject matters it covers.

At no event shall the author or Actium Publishing be liable or responsible for any loss or damage caused, or alleged to be caused, to any person or entity, directly or indirectly by the information contained in this book. In spite of the effort that has been made to ensure the accuracy, quality, currentness, validity and suitability of the information written in this book, there may be mistakes, both typographical and in content. The information in this book is not warranted or guaranteed in any way.

Product or brand names used in this book may be trade names or trade marks. These names have been used in an editorial manner without any intent to convey endorsement of or other affiliation with the name claimant. The author and the publisher express no judgment as to the validity or legal status of any such proprietary claims.

The names of some of the businesses and individuals mentioned in this book have been changed to protect their privacy.

MISTAKES, OVERSIGHTS AND FAILURES

Abe Espinal was employed as a salesman in a thriving hardware store. In 1994, as the Internet business revolution loomed on the horizon, he decided to jump on the bandwagon and start his own Internet business. Since he had a lot of experience in the hardware and tool business, it was only natural for him to choose a virtual hardware store for his first Internet-based enterprise. He worked with an Internet consultant and used a Web-site designing software to set up an eye-pleasing, efficient virtual store: there were no time-consuming graphics that would frustrate the site's visitors, and no distracting gimmicks that would annoy them. Abe had observed every rule in the Internet entrepreneur's book, and provided his customers with quick, safe and convenient ways to find what they needed on his site and order it.

Promoting the site was next. Abe had registered his Web-site with every search engine he could find online, every "What's New" directory, and every link-exchange service. He had carefully posted messages to several newsgroups, and announced the opening of his new site to hundreds of online magazines and information centers. His site offered great deals on everyday items, huge discounts on bulk purchases, and even sweepstakes. No conventional hardware store could have competed with him since he operated from a small, low-rent warehouse and had very little overhead.

Two years later, with most of the pages in his first invoice-book still left blank, he closed the business down. Today he operates a small, main-street hardware store, makes a nice living, and regrets every minute he spent on his unsuccessful online venture.

But there are tens of thousands of successful Internet entrepreneurs, some of which started their business on a shoestring, who would not agree with Espinal. They were neither smarter nor luckier, and had no more business experience or education than he had, and yet they succeeded where he failed. What they all had in common, and what Abe Espinal never did, was this:

They all remembered that their venture was a *real-world business* first, *an online* business second. They were in business to make money, not to become Internet purists.

In other words, successful Internet entrepreneurs (a.k.a. *netrepreneurs*) do not limit themselves to the online world in their efforts to promote their businesses. They combine their Internet-based business with a conventional one. They take advantage of the opportunities the online world opens before them, but do not neglect to seek such opportunities in the real, conventional world. Running a business on the Internet is not akin to playing a computer game, where all that is required of the player is to press the right keys on the keyboard, or click the mouse button. A successful Internet business does not separate itself from the real world. It is a business with two simultaneous marketing approaches: one that targets online customers and one that targets conventional, offline ones.

These are the main things that new, over-enthusiastic Internet entrepreneurs often tend to overlook:

- Their telephone

- Their fax machine

- The postal service

- Newspapers and other periodicals (paper-based)

- Word of mouth (other than through e-mail)

● Radio and television

● The local population

● Exhibitions and conventions

● Direct mail

● Networking

● Direct advertising (e.g., flyers)

● Actively soliciting sales (not necessarily by cold-calling)

● Common sense

Let's go back to Abe's online business. Where did he go wrong? The first thing he overlooked was his own city's customer base. He never published an ad in the local Yellow Pages, for instance. He also forgot that, although his business does not have a storefront, he could still take orders through the telephone, fax machine, and his mail box. He had the best deals in town — but kept it a secret from the town's residents, many of whom also log onto the Internet.

An ad in the Yellow Pages displaying his Web address would have attracted visitors to Espinal's Web site in addition to generating conventional (phone) sales. A simple message such as "For all your hardware needs, check everyone else's prices — then call us!" would have done wonders for his business.

He could also have posted small ads on neighborhood billboards, left flyers in local supermarkets, stores and other places of business, and had people hand out flyers on street corners. Taking the local population into account could have provided him with a customer base that would have allowed his business to survive through the first hard years.

Abe could have also sold his items through direct mail. A small catalog or circular would have enabled him to flaunt his strongest point

— great prices — and to bring his message to the homes of thousands of potential customers.

Not only can such conventional methods generate conventional sales (through the telephone, mail, etc.), they can also increase online traffic to a Web site:

• Many local potential customers who have an Internet connection but who have never heard of a particular Web site before may become its online customers once they see that site's Internet address in a conventional ad. This is simply promoting an Internet site offline.

• These same customers, as well as customers who do not have Internet access, will recommend this business to their out-of-town relatives and friends. Word of mouth, after all, is the most effective promotion any business could ask for.

What emerges now is a model of a successful business — not just an Internet business, but a "multi-media" one. Each element of promotion supports the others:

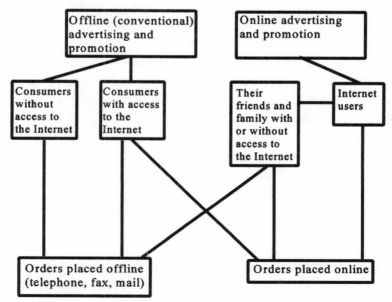

The difference between the business model described in the previous page and the one Abe actually used (sticking to online promotion only) can be compared to the difference between the development of an *isolated pawn* and that of a *pawn chain* in the game of chess. An isolated pawn is the weakest chesspiece in the game. It can be taken by almost any rival chesspiece. A pawn chain (a diagonal set of pawns which protect each other) consisting of only two such weak chesspieces can be taken by almost no one. Two pieces, or tools of the game, succeed where one cannot. Abe Espinal chose to use only one pawn when he could have utilized at least two — is there any wonder he failed?

Ignoring the Media

The following scenario is so common among Internet entrepreneurs, it can almost be considered a typical one. A creative person, who is a frustrated nine-to-five employee in a large corporation, comes up with a new idea. This can be a revolutionary device such as a mobile shower for campers, or an information product such as an how-to manual or software. This individual decides to market the product on the Internet. He sets up an impressive Internet site, with high-quality color photographs of the product and detailed descriptions of its functions. He then spends time, energy and money on online promotion through e-mail, newsgroups, search engines, etcetera. He also advertises the new site/product on high-traffic sites. Unlike Abe Espinal in the previous example, this entrepreneur *does* place ads in magazines and local periodicals, and does not forget local consumers.

Thanks to a particularly successful promotional campaign, this entrepreneur's Internet site records several hundreds of visitors per day. Encouraged and enthusiastic, he believes financial success to be just around the corner. But money never comes in. Most of the visitors to the new site turn out to be no more than curious Internet surfers with no real intention of purchasing the product. The number of actual customers is infinitesimally small.

There are a number of reasons for this:

- **People rarely search the Internet, or online search engines, for uncommon specialty products** such as mobile showers or a guide to inexpensive parking lots in the New York metropolitan area. These are simply not the products the majority of people would be looking for; rather, these are items consumers stumble across accidently and say, "Yes, I need one of those!" Since only a few people will be looking for the product by name (e.g., "mobile shower") or description, the hundreds of hours the entrepreneur had spent registering his site with various search engines and linking it to other sites would all be gone down the drain.

- **Finding the right online advertising spot in which to place ads for specialty products is hard.** Related specialty sites would more often than not be small and have few visitors. Larger sites charge a lot for displaying ads, and are often less effective since they appeal to a general audience.

But the most important reason a specialty product or an imaginative new idea fails to catch on or sell is the fact that the media does not take notice of it. While media coverage is important to every business, whether it is a retailer, a service provider or a manufacturer, it is doubly important for anyone who is trying to sell something new and original. To be interested in a new product or service, consumers have to be aware of its existence. Trying to educate the public through magazine ads or radio/TV commercials can be very expensive. The media, whose job it is to report news to the public, will do this for free. The exposure enthusiastic journalists or editors can give a new product or a Web site can be far greater than what ads or commercials may achieve. Also, people tend to believe an independent editorial or magazine column more than they do an ad or a commercial.

Working with the media is the most important and cost-effective aspect of promoting an online business. For some businesses, as with the above example, it is crucial, but for *all* businesses it is a necessity. Ignoring the media is one of the most common mistakes new Internet entrepreneurs make.

Mail-Order and the Internet

What happens to the entrepreneurs whose online businesses fail? Some, having recognized that their fledgling online business will not generate a decent income any time soon, interpret this as a vote of "not interested in your products/services" from consumers, and they abandon the business altogether. Others switch to mail-order. Mail-order entrepreneurs begin by placing small classified ads in relevant magazines. When the ads produce some results (this rarely happens overnight) and the money begins to trickle in, they begin to place larger display ads.

But there is also a third group. These are the entrepreneurs who never abandon their online business. Yes, they do begin to market their products or services through mail-order, but their magazine ads also mention the Internet site's Web address (URL). The immediate result, of course, is that the number of visitors to the site grows, but the real important development is that *these* visitors are potential customers — not just bored Internet surfers.

Small display ads (1/9th or 1/12th of a page) can offer the reader only a glimpse of the product. However, those readers who visit the site can find all the information they need, as well as pictures, testimonials and an e-mail address to which they could send their questions or comments. The Internet site thus becomes a catalog, and allows the entrepreneur to hit his potential customers with far more information and sales material than a magazine ad by itself ever could. The mail-order ad works in tandem with the site. Once again, a pawn chain is formed, where every element of promotion supports the others.

These "combined-warfare" entrepreneurs prevail. In a year or two, they are likely to have a mail-order and an Internet business whose combined income is greater than it would have been if both businesses had been run separately.

Measuring Success Online

A successful Internet site is not necessarily one that attracts many visitors. For example, it is common knowledge among book publishers that a site's success is measured not in the number of visitors it has, nor even in the number of books it had sold *online*, but rather in the number of books had it sold, period. Some of the most successful book publishers sell only one or two books a day through their sites — not a huge success by any measure. However — these sites sell many more books indirectly, by referring visitors to bookstores (whether "real" stores or virtual ones such as Amazon.com) and by helping generate media coverage. Such Internet sites are considered *promotional sites*. In other words, they are not expected to produce direct sales, but long-term indirect results. These successful publishers have found that **not** forcing customers to buy books directly from their sites would support, rather than hurt, their titles' sales.

Almost any Internet-based business can be a success. Hundreds of thousands, if not millions of people are making a good living online. All it takes is to think "business" instead of "Internet"; to seize every opportunity, not just online ones. This book will teach you how to develop imaginative, flexible business thinking, and how to make your **business** (with an Internet site) — not just your **Internet site** — a success.

2

INTERNET BASICS

The Internet is a relatively new concept. Although it has been in existence in one form or another since the early seventies, it was made available to the general public just in 1991. A new and dynamic market, the Internet is still in its formative years. Virtually all companies or individuals doing business there are fledgling Internet entrepreneurs with still a lot to learn (including those that are backed by century-old corporations).

Birth

The Internet's forefather was the ARPANET. This precursor was developed in the early seventies for the Advanced Research Projects Agency (hence the ARPA in the ARPANET) of the Defense Department. The ARPANET incorporated a new system of communication called *packet switching*. Packet switching breaks down transmitted information into small bundles of data that travel independently of one another.

Why is this an advantage? Let us suppose that two people are talking to each other on the telephone (Figure 2-1). The one connecting telephone line is the only way for transmitting data (in this case — electrical signals) from one phone to the other. What happens if someone cuts this line? This, of course, would bring the conversation to an abrupt end.

But what if, instead of one direct line, the phone company were to connect these two individuals through operators who could choose from many lines (Figure 2-2)? Cutting one, or even several lines, would not end the conversation as long as the operators can switch to alternate routes and continue the connection between the two parties.

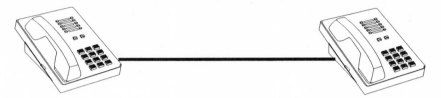

Figure 2-1   A connection through one telephone line.

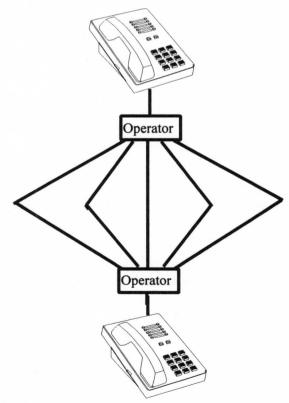

Figure 2-2   A connection through one line with alternate routes.

Packet switching works in quite the same way: the information sent from one party (or computer) is broken into independent sections called *data packets*. Each packet carries with it the address of its destination, and its sequence information (its "place in the line"). On their way, the data packets pass through packet switches, which are high-speed computers known as routers. With their help, the packets then find the best routes to their destination, and once there, they are reassembled into one message which can be seen as digital information or converted into voice, pictures, etc.

If you have Windows on your PC, you can easily trace the route that packets are taking from an Internet site to your computer. After you log onto the Internet, click on PROGRAMS and select MSDOS, which will open a DOS window without leaving the Windows environment. At the "C:\" prompt, type: TRACERT, a space, and then the address of the site ("domain name.com"). Don't include the general prefix http://. For example:

TRACERT Actium1.com.

Your computer will display the site's IP address (see page 22) and all the packet switches (hops) between this site and your computer.

Packet switching is a form of communication that by design is difficult to disturb — even if a large number of communication lines all over the country were to collapse. Even in the event of a nuclear war.

The ARPANET was conceived to ensure communication between government agencies and military installations at all times. However, using packet switching also provided other advantages. Since there is no direct line between the parties/computers, the calling party only pays for the cost of the call to the first packet switch, which is usually a local call. As a result, a person from Boston could communicate with her colleague in Los Angeles, or even Tokyo, for the price of a local call. For research and educational institutions, who thrive on the free exchange of ideas, the potential was enormous. Under their pressure, the government opened the ARPANET to colleges, universities and scientific institutes.

With the end of the cold war, the ARPANET was replaced by the NSFNET, which is maintained by the National Science Foundation. In 1991, its gates were opened to the general public. The NSFNET is the main backbone of the Internet as we know it today. The Internet is not one network, but rather a network of networks. To understand how this super network works, we must look first at basic network models.

There are two kinds of computer networks:

1. **LANs (Local Area Networks).** These small networks usually belong to corporations or small government agencies. The computers are connected directly to one another and are often located within the same building.

2. **WANs (Wide Area Networks).** Spread over long distances, sometimes even spanning the globe, these networks often use packet switching (instead of a direct connection between computers) and include several LANs.

The Internet consists of LANs, WANs and individual computers. To connect to the Internet, a computer or network needs to use *TCP/IP protocol.* This is a set of rules governing the transfer of data between computers on the Internet. The operating system of the Internet, which includes this TCP/IP protocol, is called UNIX. UNIX is to the Internet what DOS is to PCs.

The Internet is composed of the following networks (Figure 2-3):

• **Backbone networks.** The NSFNET is the best known of these, but there are others, which belong to government organizations and research institutes. They can be regarded as the caretakers of the Internet.

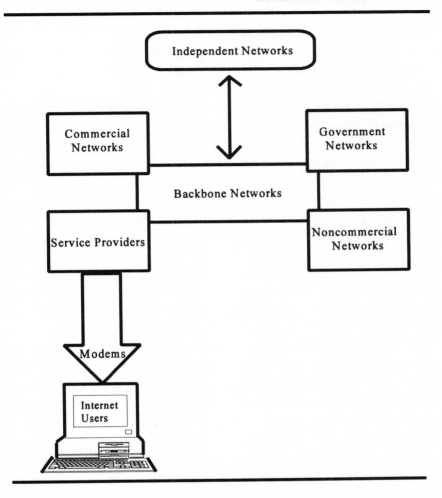

Figure 2-3 The structure of the Internet

- **Commercial networks.** These are businesses with a direct connection to the Internet. Almost every large corporation has such a direct connection, as well as many smaller companies.

- **Service providers.** These, too, are businesses with a direct connection to the Internet, but their main function is allowing individuals with PCs and modems to log onto the Internet through their link (see next page).

- **Noncommercial networks.** These belong to educational institutes, regional institutes, foreign governments and organizations, etc.

- **Independent networks with a gateway to the Internet.** While these networks are *online* (you can reach them with a modem/digital line), they are not an integral part of the Internet, and have their own inner circle of subscribers. Many of them, however, allow their users to connect to the Internet. Examples of such networks are America Online (AOL), CompuServe and Prodigy. They can be thought of as service providers with networks of their own.

Individuals log onto the Internet through commercial service providers or independent networks. Most of them connect to their service providers through a conventional telephone line, often the same line they use for making phone calls. This is convenient, but phone (voice) lines have one major drawback: they can handle analog data (electric signals with varying frequencies) but not digital data (comprised of zeros and ones). To convert digital data, which computers recognize, into analog data and back, Internet subscribers use modems. Modems vary in speed. Currently, the fastest modems around have a speed of 56Kbps, which means that they can convert data at a rate of 56,000 bytes per second. In case you are wondering, this is considered slow, especially when you want to view a Web site that contains pictures or moving graphics. Modems often require Internet users to wait 15 to 30 seconds for elaborate Web pages to appear in full on their computer screens.

Not everyone who connects to the Internet uses modems and telephone lines. There are also high-speed communication lines that were designed to handle digital data. The most common of these digital lines is the ISDN line (usually with a speed of 128Kbps), which many local phone companies now install for a nominal charge (these lines usually carry a monthly maintenance fee, though). Another way of connecting to the Internet is through cable modems, offered by some cable TV companies. These allow for considerably higher transfer speeds (3000Kbps and up), but require fiber optic lines. A new technology called DSL (Digital Subscriber Line) allows for speeds that are almost as high as the cable lines' through conventional telephone lines. However, it will be some time before these technologies are available to all Internet users.

Clients and Servers

Anyone who connects to the Internet, and who uses TCP/IP protocol (don't worry — it is included in the software package you get from your service provider or PC vendor) is known as a *client*. Clients, which are usually referred to as *Internet users* or *subscribers*, can communicate with host computers. Unlike clients, these hosts (a.k.a. servers) have a presence online — they can be reached online.

Who is a *host*? Every Internet site you can reach, whether it belongs to a large corporation, a government agency, or an individual is a host. On its Internet site, a host can store digital information in many forms:

➤ Text

➤ Pictures

➤ Sound

➤ Video clips

➤ Special commands (e.g., links that transfer the user to a different site)

The information stored by a host can be available to anyone, or limited to certain people. The information on a Web site is usually available to all visitors. The information on an e-mail server, on the other hand, is not. When one Internet user sends another user an e-mail message, this message is not sent directly to that user (being a client, he has no online presence and therefore no ability to receive messages) but to his e-mail server. When this person wants to read his e-mail messages, he has to log in with his e-mail server and download the messages from there. Internet users with an e-mail box do not really have an e-mail box, but rather an account with an e-mail server. The information on this e-mail server is not available to everyone, but to the owners of e-mail boxes alone.

Every Internet host has an Internet address, called an *IP (Internet Protocol) address*. This is a series of four numbers that looks like this:

123.45.678.9.

If you are connected to the Internet, you have probably noticed that the addresses you key in to reach an Internet site look nothing like this numerical monstrosity, and are in fact composed of letters. These lettered addresses are called *domain names* (see the following pages for examples of typical domain names). Each domain name is connected to its own IP address. Why do we use domain names instead of directly keying in the numerical IP address? There are a few reasons:

- It is much easier to remember names than long combinations of numbers.

- Using domain names allows businesses to use their trade name in their Internet address, and therefore makes it easier for a potential customer to find them.

- Much like a telephone number, an IP address belongs to the physical location it is assigned to, rather than to its owner. Internet sites sometimes change their server, or the computer their site is stored in. Using an IP address alone would have meant having to change it quite often.

In a nut shell, using an IP address as the only Internet address would be akin to a corporation listing itself in the Yellow Pages under its telephone number alone, with no company name.

INTERNET TOOLS

Internet sites are not birds of a feather. Internet servers, or hosts, can present themselves to visitors in several different ways. You can establish a presence online by using any of the following Internet tools.

E-mail

E-mail (electronic mail) is a tool that allows Internet users to send and receive messages (usually text). While having an e-mail box cannot be regarded as having an Internet site, many entrepreneurs and business people use their e-mail address as an important business tool. E-mail is being used in business in three main ways:

- **As a communication tool.** E-mail has become a real, legitimate alternative to phone conversations, faxes and land mail.

- **As a tool for disseminating information to potential customers.** For example, a manufacturer of photographic equipment may choose to include the e-mail address of a *mailbot* (a program that replies automatically to inquiries) which would send curious photographers information about the firm's new flash via e-mail.

- **As a tool for unsolicited promotion.** Although this is in direct contrast to the general Internet mentality and etiquette (a.k.a. *netiquette*), many businesses still practice this inexpensive method of in-your-face advertising. More on this in page 89.

E-mail addresses are composed of the e-mail box owner's account name (often the person's own name), the "at" sign (@) and a domain name (usually the name of the service provider). A typical e-mail address looks like this:

george@abcde.com (pronounced George at abcde dot com)

The zone name *com* identifies the nature of the addressee. These are the most common zone names you are likely to encounter:

com   commercial organization

edu   educational organization

mil   military

gov   government

org   non-profit and research organizations

net   network administration and service organization

int   international organizations

Foreign countries list the country code after the zone name (usually this does not apply to U.S. servers). For example:

jerry@ptbac.net.uk

FTP

FTP (File Transfer Protocol) is a program that allows the transfer of computer files over the Internet. Such files can contain images, video clips, sound recordings, software and even text arranged in a graphic form (e.g., forms and documents). When users reach an FTP site, they download the files that are stored at that site, and may save them to their own hard disk. Public FTP sites, which allow everyone to share their files, are called *anonymous FTPs*. A typical FTP address looks like this:

http://ftp.bradley.edu

Gopher

A *Gopher* site is simply an online menu (see Figure 2-4). Visitors select the item they need, and click on the icon to its left. Such items can be FTP files, which the visitor can download, or any of a variety of other features: pictures, text, database searches, links to other sites, other gophers, an e-mail box and more.

This variety allows Gopher sites to function as virtual storefronts. Potential customers who visit such a site can search and view information on a specific product, or view pictures, place an order, and contact the company's customer service department. Most Gophers, however, belong to universities and research institutes. Businesses usually prefer to set up their business presence on the World Wide Web (see ahead) rather than Gopherspace. A typical Gopher address looks like this:

yaleinfo.yale.edu

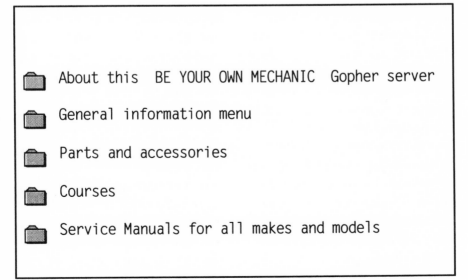

Figure 2-4 A typical Gopher site

Many Gophers are linked to each other in a directory hierarchy that is usually arranged by subject. While searching for specific items or files, the user may navigate through several different Gophers that belong to separate organizations. You can reach Gopherspace (a collective term applied to all Gopher servers) through Web sites such as Global Commerce Link:

http://www.mac.net/net2/internet/internetrsc.html

You can also use this site to reach other Internet tools that are described in this chapter, such as FTP sites, Veronica and Archie.

The World Wide Web

The *World Wide Web*, a.k.a. WWW or "the Web," can best be described as Gopher in disguise. You still have the menu/directory that can link you to any type of file, image, search engine, or even other sites, but *this* menu can look as though it was created by an artist. For example, instead of the words: "Contact Us" which a visitor to the site can click on to pop open an e-mail program, a Web site would feature a picture of a mail box that performs the same function. Instead of a boring Gopher menu featuring a business site (Figure 2-4), this same menu (in color, and written in fancier fonts) can be posted on a graphically pleasing page complete with pictures, sounds or even animation (Figure 2-5).

All Web sites have at least one home page. A home page is normally where the site's menu is located, although sometimes it only contains the corporate logo of the site's owner, and a brief description of the company's history and products. In such cases, the home page provides a link to a menu page. Figure 2-5 is, of course, a home page.

The media coverage of the Internet tends to concentrate mainly on the Web. Reason? What TV producer would not rather show a colorful and attractive site than a few dull lines of text? With this slanted media coverage, is there any surprise that many, if not most, of

How to save hundreds of dollars a year in car maintenance and repair costs

- You and your car: an overview

  General information about car maintenance and repair

- Buying parts and accessories

  Where to look for them

- Courses

- Service manuals

  All makes and models

- Links

  Find Similar sites

- Articles

- Contact us

Figure 2-5 A typical Web site

the people who are not yet connected to the Internet have come to believe that the Internet and the Web are one and the same?

And, in a way, they're right. Virtually all new commercial Internet sites today have a Web presence. The Web has a lot going for it, and only one (temporary) problem: speed. A much larger amount of data is needed to transfer images, sounds and animation online than is needed for simple text. In the future, it will probably be commonplace to visit Web sites and watch full-screen video clips that greet visitors and give them a small "orientation speech." However, until transmission speeds improve and fast connections become widely available, Web site designers must take the speed factor into account when designing a site. This means small graphics and animation, a text-only option, etc. (see page 42).

The Web seems destined to become the future of the Internet, and we might even say with a some certainty that it is also the present. The average Internet user divides his time between three major Internet tools: e-mail, newsgroups and the Web. Visiting FTP and Gopher sites is seldom on the Internet rookie's agenda. As the first generation of glitzy, over-designed Web pages gives way to new sites that make better use of text and plain, simple designs, it becomes apparent that the Web is here to stay. For you as a business operator, the Web is the most interesting facet of the Internet. Reasons?

- **The Web allows entrepreneurs an almost limitless versatility:** they can display text, sound clips, video clips, graphics, animation, photographs and more. They can also allow their customers to fill order-forms, download files and make payments online.

- **Advertisers prefer to work only with Web sites.** Ads are nearly always of a graphic nature (rather than plain text) and so is the Web.

- **The Web gets all the media attention.** As far as most of the public (including your potential customers) is concerned, it is the only game in town.

- **Creativity is central to entrepreneurial success, and creativity and Web site design go hand in hand.** The Web allows you to distinguish yourself from your competitors, to create a unique virtual business front that nobody else has, and to constantly change and experiment with new ideas.

Setting up a Web presence is a good idea even if you do not sell anything directly online (e.g., if you use your site for promotional purposes only). A Web site address is also known as a *URL* (Universal Resource Locator), and typically looks like this:

http://www.actium1.com

There are, however, Web sites that do not have the prefix WWW before their URL, so don't add WWW automatically to any URL you type in your browser!

For more information on setting up a site on the Web, see Chapter 3.

Newsgroups

Also known as Usenet newsgroups, or discussion groups, these are the Internet's bulletin boards. You can't establish a lasting presence on a newsgroup (unless you start your own), but many entrepreneurs have nonetheless learned how to make an efficient, beneficial use of them in promoting their business.

There are tens of thousands of discussion groups, each aimed at a specific audience and covering one or more topics. Two examples are: alt.agriculture.fruit and alt.drugs.caffeine. Anyone can post messages to a newsgroup. The vast majority of postings are text files, but it is also possible to attach a picture, a sound recording, and even a video clip to a newsgroup message. Posted messages remain on the newsgroup only for a few days, and then they expire. Newsgroups fall under several categories that are denoted by the prefix attached to the newsgroup's subject word.

The most common newsgroup categories are:

alt	Alternative. These newsgroups do not belong to any other category, and may range from the weird to the offensive.
bionet	Biology
biz	Business
comp	Computers
k12	Teachers newsgroups (kindergarten to 12th grade)
misc	Miscellaneous subjects. Sometimes these are a combination of several subjects within the same newsgroup.
rec	Recreational activities
sci	Science
soc	Social issues
talk	Ongoing newsgroup conversations and debates — text messages only.

Mailing Lists (online)

Mailing lists are similar in function to newsgroups, with the exception that Internet users have to subscribe to them first in order to read them, and that the articles are then sent directly to their e-mail addresses. One well-known mailing list program is ListServe (short for List Service). Whenever a message is posted to a ListServe group, it is received by all subscribers. Some mailing lists (as well as some newsgroups) are moderated: someone sorts out the incoming e-mail messages and decides which ones to post for subscribers. Mailing lists are an excellent tool for businesses who want to keep in touch with their customers by sending them updates on new products or services.

Chat

Chat programs allow Internet users to converse with other Internet users in real time by using either text or vocal communications. You can carry a telephone-style conversation with someone from Japan, for example, and be charged only for the local connection to your Internet server (in other words, it would be a local call). Some businesses have set up their own chat lines, which are accessible from their Web site. These chat lines are usually moderated, and a customer service representative takes customers' questions in real time. These private chat programs are rapidly replacing the telephone as the preferred form of real-time communication between customers and online businesses, and nowadays entire customer service departments rely on them.

Less Common Internet Tools

As mentioned before, most Internet users today are not computer buffs, and they use only three main online tools: e-mail, the Web and newsgroups. However, there are several other tools to be found on the Internet, and although you are not likely to use them very often, it is good to know they exist.

- **WAIS** (Wide Area Information Servers). This is a program that searches a word or a string of letters in a certain database (not unlike the Window's Find command). WAIS is usually incorporated into Web sites, and the user is often unaware of its being a separate tool. It is a very important addition to sites that hold vast amounts of text, or to commercial sites with a great number of items for sale. For example, an online bookstore with a huge inventory will incorporate a WAIS tool into its Web site to help customers locate a certain title or to find an author's name. There are also independent WAIS sites on the Internet, which offer access to general databases.

- **Telnet**. The Telnet protocol is an online remote control. It allows Internet users to control a computer they connect to online as if they were sitting at that computer's keyboard. Telnet is used to search, retrieve and view files from the remote computer, and perform many other file tasks. Telnet is usually combined with other features, and is rarely presented as an independent service.

- **Archie**. Archies (short for archive) are lists of file names from FTP sites. This is basically a file-search service that allows users to find the location of the desired file by entering its name.

- **Finger.** This is a command that allows Internet users to view basic information on businesses and individuals who have chosen to store this information in a special text file (named *.plan* or *.project*). The finger command will only work, therefore, with *some* e-mail addresses. The information displayed by this command may vary from a telephone number to a price list, and may also include the person's last log-in (the last time he viewed his e-mail messages). Not every system supports finger, but you can always use services like Yahoo's list of finger gateways to view some of them. Some businesses use finger to display important information about their company to potential customers, but due to the lack of awareness of this tool's existence, it is now rarely used.

- **Veronica**. A file search service similar to Archie, with the exception that Veronica searches Gopher menus rather than FTP sites.

THE ONLINE WORLD OUTSIDE THE INTERNET

As you probably know, the Internet is not synonymous with the online world. Not every service or computer we can reach with a modem or even through the Internet itself is an integral part of the Internet. Some online systems are not directly connected to the main backbone networks that support the Internet, or even to the Internet's smaller networks. However, these independent systems (or networks) join together with Internet networks to make what we refer to as the online world (Figure 2-3). Some of these independent systems are small single PCs (BBSs) while others are huge independent networks which are online communities unto themselves.

BBS

BBS stands for Bulletin Board System. A BBS can be defined as any computer that has the following characteristics:

1. It is connected to a telephone line through a modem or a similar device.

2. It allows callers to use its software and files.

BBSs are usually single computers, as opposed to large, multi-computer networks. A BBS might be similar in content and appearance to an ordinary Internet site, but visitors would have to dial the BBS's phone number in order to reach it, because the BBS is not directly connected to the Internet. Some BBSs can be reached through the Internet via special servers, however. BBS lists are available at:

http://aug3.augsburg.edu/files/bbs_list

Independent Networks

These include: CompuServe, America Online, Delphi and Prodigy. These independent networks are online communities in their own right. Some have their own online malls, magazines and just about every other service users can find on the Internet. However, since their subscribers are relatively few, the amount of resources that are normally available to Internet users cannot be matched by these networks. For this reason, most of them now allow their subscriber unlimited access to the Internet. For example, subscribers to America Online (AOL) can visit sites (similar in appearance to Web sites) that are within the AOL network, but they can also browse regular Internet sites that are located outside AOL.

The Independent networks usually send their subscribers special software that contain graphics, fonts, sound clips, etc. Subscribers download these images to their computer hard drive. When these subscribers visit a site that is located within the independent network itself, the special software allows them to download images or sounds very quickly, because many of these images are already stored on the subscriber's computer. In other words, instead of downloading tremendous volume of data in order to display images, these subscribers need only download a set of instructions that would tell their computers where to place images from their own image library. As a result, the transfer speed of images is much higher than that of the Web, and graphics appear almost instantaneously on the user's screen. The trade off, of course, is the small graphic variety — only a certain number of image combinations can be offered by the independent networks' software, and constant updates are required for new images and fonts.

3

STARTING A BUSINESS ONLINE

As mentioned in the previous chapter, connecting to the Internet and setting up a business presence there are two very different things. When an Internet user connects to the Internet, she does so through a service provider, which simply allows her access to the Internet, no more. This is called a dial-up account and the user can only "read" the Internet, not write her own Internet files or set up her own site (some service providers do allow subscribers to create a personal home-page with limited features, but it is not practical for business use). In contrast, a business presence online (a.k.a. a virtual storefront) requires a storage space on a computer that is accessible through the Internet. Technically, Internet sites are no more than a certain quantity of computer bytes (several megabytes for the average site). The companies that own and operate the computers which host Internet sites are called *server services.*

Server Services

Where do you find a server service? You can search for their ads in business and Internet magazines, or use the words "server service" with one of the Internet's main search engines (Infoseek, Alta Vista, Yahoo, etc.). All server services can be reached online. Many of them display their rates, terms and a list of their services online, allowing for an easy, quick comparison. Unlike service providers, server services are usually small companies with no more than several hundred customers each, and it is possible to negotiate a package deal with some of them. Another difference between server services and service providers is geographical flexibility: service providers — your connection to the Internet — have to be physically located in your near-vicinity so that calls placed to them through your modem would be local calls. Server services, which only host your site on their computer, do not need to be contacted through a direct telephone line, and can therefore be located anywhere in the world as far as you are concerned. You can choose any server service you want to work with regardless of where you live — there is no need to compromise.

What should you consider when looking for a server service?

- **Rates.** Naturally, rates vary according to the type and size of the site you wish to set up. For a small-to-medium site with no special features, the monthly rate today is $25-$50. Expect to pay more if you anticipate a high volume of traffic to your site (the server service would have to give your site a high-speed connection). Many server services charge a one time set-up fee in addition to the monthly fee. The set-up fee is usually no higher than twice the monthly fee.

- **Customer service.** Although you cannot expect the server service to teach you how to start an Internet business, or how to run your site, they should be able to answer all your technical questions. Setting up a site requires the transfer of files (which would become Web pages) from your PC to the server service's computer (this is called *uploading*), and minor difficulties are bound to ensue during the first few months.
    The server service will let you download a special FTP software that would enable you to upload and manage your site's files from your computer (or they will refer you to a site from which you can download such software). This is a very simple process, similar to managing files (copying, deleting) on your Windows or equivalent file manager. **Never use a server service that requires you to send them your files on floppy disks!** This

is time-consuming and does not allow the flexibility of uploading files through your modem.

The customer service department of most server services can be reached by phone. However, since your server service, unlike your service provider, might be located on the other side of the country, prolonged telephone conversations might prove expensive. To avoid excessive long distance charges, make sure your server service also offers customer service through e-mail or chat programs.

- **Range of service.** Your server service must be able to support all the tools your online business might need. For example, if you want a secure server for credit card transactions (see page 52), your server service must be able to support this.

- **Domain name use.** The domain name you choose for your site (see page 22) is not necessarily the URL your server service will allow you to use. For instance, if you have a Web site and your domain name is "superdeals2000," your URL should read: http://www.superdeals2000.com.   However, if you had chosen a low-rate package for your site, you might find that your site's URL is:

    http://www.superdeals2000.com/yourcode

    The server service in this example has set up your site as a subdirectory of another site. Although this is by no means a problem, the longer URL is harder to remember and less efficient for advertising use. Some server services would not let you use your domain name at all, and instead require you to use their own. **Do not use them.**

- **No hidden fees.** Make sure there are no charges for updating your site, or for other miscellaneous services you do not need.

- **E-mail services.** The server service should give you at least one e-mail box, preferably with your own domain name. Many server services also offer virtual e-mail addresses (e-mail addresses that forward messages to your "real" e-mail box).

- **Auto responders.** Make sure the server service can provide auto responders for you should you need them (see page 43).

- **Beware of gimmicks.** For example, many server services offer to register your site with several search engines free of charge. Since you will have to promote your site anyway, this should not be a factor in considering whether to use the service server (not to mention that they are probably not going to do as good a job at this as you would).

ALTERNATIVES TO USING A SERVER SERVICE

Even though most Internet businesses choose a server service to host their site, there are other ways to set up a business presence on the Internet.

A Direct, Dedicated Connection

Connecting directly to the Internet (as a server, not a user) really means that your site can be reached from the Internet through a special line that only your site uses. To allow this, you would need a UNIX workstation (UNIX is the Internet's operating system), a computer that would store your site, and a dedicated connection. As the name suggests, a dedicated connection means that you do not share your Internet connection with anyone, unless you decide to become a server service and charge others for using it. The dedicated line is usually a high-speed digital line such as ISDN, T1 or T3. A direct connection to the Internet also requires the use of special equipment and software. The total cost? Probably no less than $10,000 if you don't rely too heavily on hired experts.

A direct connection is a good idea only for large businesses that expect very high traffic in their site, and for entrepreneurs who wish to open a server service or an Internet mall (see next section). For small entrepreneurs, and even for most multi-million dollar corporations, a server service would be able to provide all the necessary hardware and services required to set up a presence on the Internet.

Entrepreneurs who need a dedicated connection to the Internet, and who do not possess the know-how required to operate one, should consider leasing this connection from a server service. Some of them offer this service for $1,000 to $3,000 a month.

Online Malls

Online malls are similar to server services, with the exception that a mall plays an active role in promoting the businesses it hosts. An online mall hosts anywhere between a few dozen to a few hundred virtual shops. When you set up a site through an online mall, you should expect more services than would be available through a server service. These additional services might include:

- **Listing your site with the mall's main directory**, which is available to anyone who visits the mall.

- **Help in conducting your business.** For example, the mall should take care of secure credit-card transactions for you.

- **The mall should promote itself on an ongoing basis**. The more potential customers there are who visit the mall, the more likely it is that some of them will visit your site. Well-established malls attract hundreds of thousands of hits (visits) per day.

The clear advantage of setting up shop with an online mall is that, in addition to the potential customers that your own promotion brings to your site, a large number of visitors will find you through the mall

— visitors who might not have otherwise known about your site. There are, however, two points to consider:

- When a visitor stops by a conventional strip mall, he is exposed to all sorts of stores. Even if his intended goal is to purchase a pair of jeans, he is involuntarily window-shopping as he walks through the mall. In addition to the pair of jeans, this customer is likely to purchase various other items from different stores — shoes, music CDs, a magazine, etc. The same visitor to an online mall would simply use the site's directory to view *only* the (virtual) clothing stores. Impulse buys are thus reduced to a minimum.

- An online mall has practically no physical limit to the number of shops it can host. Unless your online mall has strict rules about the number of businesses of the same type that can rent a space there, you may find yourself dealing with lots of competition.

There is also a different kind of online mall that does not host sites, but merely provides links to the businesses listed in its directory. To use the services of this kind of mall, you would need to set up a site with a server service first.

Connecting through Non-Internet Networks

Independent networks such as America Online also offer server services to businesses. Often, they offer better deals than regular server services, and help you design your site. Make, sure, however, that they comply with the requirements listed on pages 36-38.

You can also use a BBS (Bulletin Board System) for your business presence. A BBS is simply a computer (often a PC) with a modem, a telephone line and a special communications software. Once users call up a BBS and gain access to it, they can run the BBS computer as if they were sitting at its keyboard (retrieve files and messages, etc.). Although some BBSs can be reached through special Internet tools, it is far easier for Internet users to reach Internet sites than BBSs. Making it harder for your potential customers to find and reach your site is probably not a good business tactic, and for this reason alone, it is best to ignore BBSs for commercial sites.

Domain Name

Every site on the Internet has a domain name. The domain name is really an Internet trade name of sorts, and it is integrated into your Internet address. For example, if your domain name is "5dollarbargains" and you have a Web site, your URL would be: http://www.5dollarbargains.com

The authority responsible for assigning domain names is called the InterNIC. To choose a domain name for your business, go to:

http://rs.internic.net/cgi-bin/whois

Type in your proposed name to see if it is already taken (you can also call the InterNIC at 703-742-4777). If the name is not taken, you can register it with them as your domain name. You can do so by contacting the InterNIC directly, or by submitting the name through your server service. The current fee is $100.

Remember that trade names supersede domain names, and you may not use another business's registered trade name even if that business does not have an Internet site. Early Internet entrepreneurs who registered household trade names as domain names for their businesses often found themselves entangled in losing legal battles with the rightful owners of the names.

Your domain name will remain the same no matter how many times you change server services. Remember — even if the server service has registered the domain name for you, it is *your* property.

You can also set up a site without a domain name of your own. Server services will gladly lend you their own domain name. Of course, in such a case, the domain name would not be yours and must be changed should you switch server services.

Your Internet Site

Today it is safe to say that a Web site is a must for Internet entrepreneurs. Even if you are planning a Gopher or an FTP site, it is a good idea to have a parallel Web site. The Web has so many advantages for the Internet entrepreneur, it simply cannot be ignored. Its main problem is speed — how quickly will your Web pages appear on Internet users' screens? In the future this problem will be solved by faster connections. Until then, and until such high-speed connections are available to *most* Internet users, there are many other ways to combat the speed problem:

- **Smaller graphics.** Use small images and icons instead of large pictures that take a quarter or more of the screen. Smaller images take a much shorter time to download.

- **Limited animation.** Animation is a good idea when done with small images, but large, complicated ones require a substantial download time. Avoid them. The same applies to video clips that play automatically whenever an Internet user visits the site.

- **A text-only option.** If you must use slow downloading graphics, provide a text-only option for visitors to your site. Users who do not want to wait for the images to download will appreciate it if they can link to a text-only page. Many Internet users use their browsers' commands to stop images from downloading, anyway.

- **As a rule of thumb,** always think twice before incorporating into your site any feature, tool or gimmick that may slow its downloading time.

Remember — even when a new generation of modems or high-speed cables makes its debut, the vast majority of Internet users will continue to use the older generation of modems for months or even years. When you visit your own site in order to evaluate its downloading speed, don't use a state of the art modem with cutting edge technology. Use the modem *most* Internet users have.

Using Other Internet Features — E-mail

Once you have set up your Web site, you might want to use other Internet tools for your online business presence. The most important of these tool is e-mail. You can use e-mail to conduct business online in two ways:

- **As a correspondence tool.** E-mail is a virtual conduit for incoming and outgoing data. You can use it for customer service, to handle customers' requests, to disseminate information about your products or services, and as a cheap, convenient substitute for telephone, fax, and land mail.

- **To reply to inquiries automatically.** Combining the versatility of e-mail with the time-saving automation of auto responders will significantly improve your ability to handle a large number of customers. Auto responders, a.k.a. mailbots, are programs that send an automatic reply to anyone who sends them a message. For example, let's assume that an entrepreneur has opened a virtual music shop. CDs, cassettes, and music videos are displayed on her Web site and are available to every visitor. However, the complete selection is spread over a very large number of Web pages, arranged by subject. What happens when a potential customer wants to view the whole list (several hundreds of titles) at a glance? An auto responder would allow such a customer to send a blank e-mail message to one of the site's e-mail addresses, and to receive, in a matter of seconds, the complete list directly to his e-mail address.

Now, let's suppose that this individual wants to receive only the full list of Rock & Roll CD titles. No problem. The auto responder can be programmed to handle such demands. Instead of sending it a blank e-mail message, the customer will send the auto responder a message with the words "Rock & Roll" in the subject line. The auto responder will reply with the appropriate list.

To make your customers' lives a little easier, you may want to use several auto responders (each with their own e-mail address) instead of one responder that would requires different keywords (subjects) for different replies. For example, one auto responder will send users (who sent it a blank message) only the list of Rock & Roll titles, a second responder will send users only classical music titles, and so on. Most server services will allow you to set up as many auto responders as you want for little or no fee.

> Auto responders are not the appropriate platform for plugging your business. People who request information should receive exactly what they asked for, or your business will be labeled a *spammer* (someone who uses unethical, unsolicited promotion).

Using Other Internet Features — Online Mailing Lists

Mailing lists work in a very similar way to auto responders. The difference is that, with a mailing list, the person who makes an inquiry is automatically subscribed to an online bulletin service which continues to send messages on a regular basis instead of just a one-time single reply. If we will take the previous example of a virtual music shop, a mailing list can be used by that entrepreneur to send customers updates on new titles or events.

There is another type of mailing list, which allows subscribers to actively participate. The virtual music shop, for example, can use it to allow customers/visitors to interact, exchange information, and share experiences. A representative of the business, who is also the list's moderator, should intervene with advice or information whenever necessary. This is a great tool for building a solid customer base.

Using Other Internet Features — Newsgroups

Newsgroups work in a similar way to the second type of mailing list described above, but they tend to be more independent of the business that started them. Posting messages to newsgroups is easier, but they are harder for the moderator to control. Newsgroups are a great tool for promotion (see Chapter 5).

Using Other Internet Features — Chat Programs

Unlike mailing lists or newsgroups, chat programs work in real time. Internet users reply to messages immediately and create a real live conversation (mostly in text form, although vocal chat programs are widely available today). Messages roll off the screen within minutes, and cannot be read by someone who logs in later as they could be in a newsgroup (where messages are posted for several days). To moderate or monitor a chat program, you would have to have a full-time employee assigned to this job.

Using Other Internet Features — FTP

Having an FTP site (which can be reached from your Web site) would serve a purpose somewhat similar to having an auto responder. However, unlike auto responders, which only allow you to send text messages to your customers, an FTP site would let them download files of any type: video and audio clips, pictures and especially software. Of course, some of these files could also be attached to e-mail messages, but this is more complicated and time-consuming than allowing your customers to download them directly from your site.

If you only have a few files you wish your customers to download, you may incorporate them into your Web site instead of lumping them together in a special directory of their own. A good example of software that you may want your customers to download are programs that allow them to view certain features of your site, such as audio or video clips. Since only a few people can write software themselves, this would mean linking your site to the FTP site of the software creator (to your customers it would seem that they download the software directly from your site, however).

Using Other Internet Features — Gopher

Should you bother with a Gopher site? In most cases, the answer is no. Few Internet users today surf Gopherspace. However, if your potential customers are students or people who use old browsers and earlier model computers (as is the case with Internet users from Third-World countries), you may want to consider setting up such a site, which would mirror your Web site.

Designing Your Internet Site and Making It Work

In the past, knowledge of *HTML* was required to design Web pages. HTML (Hypertext Markup Language) is the script that enables the layout of Web pages and the use of *hot keys* (text or images that give an Internet command when they are clicked on). Back then (early nineties — a long, long time ago in Internet terms), Internet entrepreneurs had but two options: learn HTML or hire an expert. These were the golden days of HTML artists, with rates averaging $100 an hour. The party was quickly over, however, with the advent of off-the-shelf Web page authoring software such as Microsoft FrontPage and Corel Word Perfect. Experts' rates have gone down steeply, and today you can easily find an HTML artist for less than $30 an hour. The question is, do you really need them?

In most cases, no. Web page authoring software usually sell for about $100, do not require you to learn HTML, and will serve you for many years to come. While it is true that you'll need some time to get the hang of it (a few hours to a few days), don't forget that you will gain valuable hands-on experience which will make the design of future Web pages a cinch (and you *will* have to create or update Web pages on a regular basis).

However, this software by itself may not always be enough, and you may need to consult other people. You may need some assistance, for example, when setting up forms for receiving payment online. This doesn't mean that you would have to hire experts. In most cases, your server service or credit card processor will be able to help. Even if you do hire experts eventually, you will not need them to design your site for you, but only to address a specific problem.

Images, pictures and animation for your site can be obtained in three ways:

- **By creating them yourself,** either with a special drawing software, or the conventional way — by using your camera or hand drawings. To convert paper-based images to digital files, you will need a scanner, which can be purchased today for as little as $80-$200.

- **By using copyright-free artwork,** which can easily be obtained in any software store. Competition in this field has driven prices down, and you can find CD-ROMs containing hundreds or even thousands of images or photographs for as little as $15-$20.

- **By picking them up from the Internet.** Once you make sure the image is not copyrighted, or you obtain the owner's consent, simply use the Save File command in your browser to save the image to your hard disk. If you are copying text, it is enough to highlight the paragraph you need and then use your PC's Copy and Paste commands (which can usually be given by holding down ctrl+c, ctrl+v) to transfer it to your Web page authoring software.

Once your Web pages are ready, all you have to do is make them accessible to Internet users. You should be able to upload the Web page files to your server service through your modem (this is also known as "FTPing" your files). This way, you'll have full control of your Internet site, and can add or delete files in second.

At this point, your site will be up and running, but in most cases, a few days, or even weeks, will pass before all the bugs are straightened out — bad links between Web pages, pages that cannot be accessed, forms that do not work, etc. With experience, such problems will become rare.

Your Home Page

This is your site's front door and store sign. You would not enter a store whose door is covered with graffiti and whose (huge) sign tells the owner's life story in three inch fonts, would you? A home page should catch the visitor's interest, but must never give the impression that he is dealing with an amateur. Over-produced home pages reek of amateurism. The home page should meet the following requirements:

- **It must tell the visitor what your special product, service or deal is, and do so succinctly.** Internet surfers' attention span is often less than ten seconds. For example, if your site is selling books, the line "Books at Half Price!" should come even before the company's name.

- **It must provide a directory of the site, arranged by subject.** Internet users grow quickly tired of a "cute" site that leads visitors through a maze of Web pages and images before they can find what they came for in the first place.

- **It is also a good idea to include small directories on every page of your site.** This way, visitors will not have to return to the home page every time they are done with another one of the site's pages. Small directories usually appear either at the bottom of every Web page or in a special side frame.

- **Links.** Provide links to sites that deal with the same subject, or that are otherwise of interest to your visitors. Links usually appear as hypertext — Internet users click on highlighted text to be transferred to another site/page. Links enrich the information and resources on your site, and improve your chances of getting repeat visitors.

- **Search engines.** If you have a particularly large Internet site, and are afraid that visitors would get lost in the maze of directories, sub-directories and Web pages, it is a good idea to incorporate a search engine into your site which will help users find the item of their choice by typing in a keyword. Online bookstores such as Amazon.com (http://www.amazon.com) employ such search engines to help customers search for books by author's name, title or subject.

- **FAQ (Frequently Asked Questions).** Let us suppose that you are running an online pharmacy. You notice that the same questions are being asked over and over. "What's the difference between generic and brand-name drugs?" "Is it O.K. to drive when I use these pills?" "How do I know if what I have is a cold or the flu?" To save yourself hundreds of personal e-mail replies, you may want to gather the most common questions and post them (with answers) on your site. Not only will this save you a lot of time, but it will make your site much more interesting, user-friendly and helpful to the visitor.

- **Tons of useful, free information.** The Internet has a distinct advantage over all other media: unlimited space. If you have no more information on your site than a magazine ad or a TV commercial can hold, you defeat the purpose of having an Internet site. Allow visitors who are interested in your product, service or industry to learn everything they can about them. The Internet community has learned to expect that.

- **Constantly add more items and pages to your site, and update existing ones.** Change is crucial to survival online.

- **Welcome visitors'/customers' contributions** such as their advice, letters to your company, comments, etc. Active participation always encourages repeat visits. In addition, this enriches your site which will benefit from more information and first-hand experience.

- **Sound and video.** Audio and video clips will add a lot to your site, but don't force them on visitors. Internet users do not appreciate it when time-consuming video clips start playing automatically whenever they enter a site. When using audio or video files, you may want to give visitors links to sites where they can download the software that enables viewing/hearing these clips (e.g., Real Audio, Internet Wave).

- **Contact information.** Always include your business's telephone number, land address, and (if applicable) fax number.

- **Speed.** See page 42 for information on improving your site's downloading speed.

Accepting Payment Online

Paying for products and services on the Internet can be done in a number of ways, and your best bet is to allow your customers a choice between several payment methods to ensure that *everyone* will be able to do business with you.

A.   **Doing it the conventional way.** Your customer sends you a check; the check clears; you send him or her the goods. Is this what the Internet was created for? Hardly. In the first place, it takes a long time. This defeats the purpose of doing business online. It is also inconvenient. The customer might think twice before ordering something, and impulse-buys can be reduced significantly. If these two reasons alone are not enough, consider international trade. Your foreign customers would have to go to their local bank and have it issue a check drawn in U.S. dollars. In addition to the hassle, there is also a substantial fee for each of these checks. There is even worse to come — you cannot deposit such a foreign check directly to your account. Your bank will have to collect the funds first, and only then will the money be made available to you. There is usually no clearance schedule for checks drawn on foreign banks, and the process might take a very long time.

B. **C.O.D. payments.** This is probably the worst method of accepting payments online. Many, if not most merchants, do not allow their customers this option. It is expensive and requires the customer to pay a C.O.D. surcharge for every delivery. It also involves a lot of paperwork and labor.

C. **Credit cards.** Like it or not, this is the future of online payment. A lot has been said about the dangers of using credit cards over the Internet — it is nothing but a myth. Using credit cards over the telephone is no less risky. Credit card numbers can and are being stolen from conventional vendors' files and records. This is easier to do than to penetrate vendors' computers through the Internet and retrieve information from there.

However, for you as an Internet entrepreneur, it does not matter if the public's fear of using credit cards over the Internet is justified or without basis. The fear is there and that is that. It is up to the online business community to assuage consumers' fears. Online businesses must offer consumers secure ways to process credit-card transactions even if such security is redundant, because consumers must feel comfortable shopping online. Payment on the Internet must not only be safe, it must seem to be safe. There are different ways for merchants to process credit-card orders and to secure them:

- **Encrypted credit card-orders.** The account information sent by the customer is encrypted, and cannot be decrypted without a code that is known only to the merchant. There is no way for unauthorized people to obtain the credit-card information. To encrypt account information, your business's credit-card transactions must be conducted through a secure server. Contact your server service for details and rates.

- **Taking credit card information over the phone.** This is a simple, conventional method. First, set up an account with a credit-card processing company for processing *telephone* orders. Your site will refer customers who do not wish to use their cards online to a telephone number over which they can order your products. Credit-card information can also be faxed or sent through the mail.

- **First Virtual** (you can reach them at: http://www.fv.com) is a company that offers a service which is halfway between the previous method and taking orders online. Their main advantage over the method described in the previous section is that they save you the time and trouble it takes to manually process telephone orders. What this company does is simple: the customer calls them and leaves his credit-card information. They give him a code (called VirtualPin). Whenever this customer needs to order an item from an online merchant who accepts First Virtual, he needs only to give that merchant his VirtualPin over the Internet. First Virtual will send that customer an e-mail message, asking him to confirm the order he has placed with the merchant within 24 hours. If the order is confirmed, the merchant is notified and the amount is deposited to his account.

Another advantage of this method is that just about any merchant can use it. Applicants are not subjected to a thorough credit check. There are two main problems with this method, however. First, the settlement period (the time it takes funds to be deposited to your account) can be much longer than that of a conventional processing company. Secondly, there are additional fees on top of the usual credit-card processing fees. First Virtual is no substitute for accepting credit cards directly, and you should try to set up an account with a credit card processing company even if you do accept First Virtual or are using a similar service.

To be able to accept credit cards, you will have to contact a processing company. They will sell you a special software for processing credit-card transactions (at a price of $700 and up). You can also choose to take the conventional processing terminal (the type stores use) which is slightly cheaper but does not offer the same ease of use.

D. **E-cash (electronic cash).** This is a relatively new concept, which works this way: The consumer buys e-cash currency from a special bank. This electronic currency is downloaded into the consumer's special account/computer. When that consumer buys an item from an online vendor that accepts e-cash, the purchase sum is electronically deducted from his or her account. The electronic cash is then deposited to the merchant's account, from which it can be drawn as (real) cash.

Advantages

- **Security.** The customer does not use a credit card.

- **Privacy.** No one can look at your credit card statements and learn what you have bought recently, which services you have been using, and where you traveled.

Disadvantages

- **Inconvenience.** The customer has to buy e-cash from a special vendor prior to being able to use it, and must do so again whenever this e-cash credit runs out.

- **You actually have to pay *before* you buy,** and no one will pay you interest for the e-cash that is just laying there unused.

Currently, only a few, if any, of your customers will be using e-cash. Furthermore, as consumers' fear of using credit cards over the Internet is slowly assuaged, this relatively inconvenient method is likely to be even less in demand in the future.

The two main issuers of online electronic currency are:

DigiCash (http://www.digicash.com)

Cyber Cash (http://www.cybercash.com)

E.   **Checks over the telephone**. Although it is possible today for some merchants to accept checks over the telephone, this method has almost the same security problems that credit-card transactions have.

To summarize — when planning the methods of payment your site is going to offer customers, be sure you allow them a choice between at least these two options:

1. Checks or money orders.

2. Credit-cards.

Budgeting

How much is setting up an online business going to cost you? The following list will provide you with some idea of the expenses involved in establishing and running a small online business:

❑ Establishing an Internet presence through a server service:
   A set-up fee of $20-$200, plus $20-$100 a month

❑ Setting up a virtual shop on an online mall:
   A set-up fee of $0-$500, plus $5-$500 a month

❑ Web site designing:
   $100-$500, if you do the work yourself with your own
   software
   $500-$10,000, if you hire experts

❑ Other (conventional) business expenses (CPA, stationery,
   miscellaneous fees):
   $2,000-10,000 when setting up your business, *plus*
   $200-$1,000 monthly

❑ Inventory, promotion, personnel:
   varies.

The main factor in calculating your costs is hiring labor: to what degree will you have to rely on consultants and experts? If you can do most things yourself (this should not be hard for a small Internet entrepreneur), you can start out on a shoestring. Save your money for the most important item: *promotion*.

Remember — large investments do not by themselves guarantee success. An online business site, however well-designed, is not government bonds. You will have to spend time and effort as well as money.

Make a business plan. Your projected income may not justify a large investment. Remember that at best, only 1 or 2 percent of the visitors to your site are going to make a purchase, and that you cannot expect to make any net income from your site for at least six months (and often a year). A small, inexpensive Internet site that is designed to survive for years on a small budget is better than a huge, expensive site that would set you back tens of thousands of dollars and may produce the same initial results as a smaller site. You can always expand your site later if the number of visitors justifies this.

The bottom line is this: almost anyone can afford to start an Internet-based business. What you cannot invest in capital, you can more than make up for with an investment of time and effort. However, you have to be realistic and understand that any business is a fledgling, struggling business at first. It takes a long-term commitment to succeed — not just starting capital.

Entrepreneurs will make mistakes. If they start out with a few thousand dollars, they make thousand-dollar mistakes. If they start out with several millions, they make million-dollar mistakes.

4

CHOOSING YOUR PRODUCT OR SERVICE

What type of business will you start online, and what product or service will you be selling? If you already have a business, and are planning to expand to the Internet, this question is irrelevant for you. If not, the future of your online business may depend on the answer to this question.

The first thing you want to do before answering is to **forget about the Internet**. Don't worry, we'll get back to it later, but for now the important thing is to plan a successful business, not just an Internet business.

When judging the suitability of any product or service, ask yourself the following questions:

- **Can *I* sell it?** Do I have the know-how? Do I know this product's market? Can I answer customer's questions about this product, its use or functions? Can I talk about this product excitingly? Do I like this business?

- **Can I buy it?** This may seem like a stupid question, but in fact this is one of the most important aspects of running any business: getting the merchandise at the right price. Anyone can contact a watch wholesaler and buy a few hundred watches at a certain discount. The problem is getting the watches at a price low enough to undercut your competitors. For example, it is very hard to find home electronics products at good wholesale prices, and so it is nearly impossible for small entrepreneurs to compete with the large chains.

> The trick to getting good deals (wholesale) on any product is buying it in quantities greater than what you will be able to sell at retail, and then selling most of it to other retailers. For instance, if a wholesaler sells a roll of film to retailers for $4.00 in quantities of 50-100, you may be able to buy this film for $3.00 if you order 10,000 rolls. You sell 8,000 rolls to retailers for a little under $4.00 (or they will not buy from you), but the 2,000 you have left can be sold at retail for $1.00 less than your competitors. This is a win-win situation.

- **Can I sell my product via drop-shipping?** What this means is that you will not be keeping an inventory, but instead you'll forward the orders you receive to another company (wholesaler or manufacturer) who will ship the item directly to the customer. The advantages of this method are that you need very little start-up capital (no inventory) and few, if any, employees. The drawback is the relatively small profit for each unit sold — the drop-shipper's cut will include handling charges. For small Internet entrepreneurs who want a large selection of items and as little investment as possible, this may be a great solution, but beware — to survive on the Internet as a retailer you have to be *price competitive*. For more on drop-shipping, see page 176.

- **Do I have other products/services to fall back on in case my main line does not sell well?** Although it is not necessary to start a business with two types of products (e.g., hardware supplies and home improvement books), it might help a fledgling business, especially one that still needs to learn the ropes. To save money, the second line of products can be sold via drop-shipping.

Online Business Considerations

Now, let us get back to the Internet. Once the product or service you have selected passes the above conventional market's test, add the following questions to your list to determine your business's viability online:

- **Is sending the product to customers via land mail cost-effective?** Not all products are right for mail-order/Internet businesses. Furniture, for example, can be a big problem if you receive an order from Oregon and your warehouse is located in Florida.

- **Is this the kind of product people want to touch, view up close, or try out before buying?** If the answer is yes, the Internet is not the appropriate place to sell it. Examples: hi-fi sound systems, earphones, dresses.

- **Do the potential customers for this product log onto the Internet?** For example, if you sell hearing aids, you may want to invest most of your money/effort in the mail-order aspect rather than the Internet part of the business. The reason? Many more elderly people read magazines than surf the Net. Another example: if you are an immigration lawyer who specializes in representing illegal immigrants from Third-World countries, then neither the Internet nor mail-order is the right tool for you. The chances that your potential customers will reach your Web site or read your ads in American magazines are remote. However, local foreign-language newspapers may turn out to be the right vehicle for you.

- **Some products sell better than others online,** such as books, software, music CDs and computer hardware. This, however, does not necessarily reflect the future of Internet commerce. Until not long ago, the majority of Internet users were students or very young people, mostly men. The average age of Internet users is constantly rising as more and more families (especially middle-class families) become part of the online world.

- **How well do you know the Internet market for your product?** Surf the Internet as a user and visit your competitors' sites. What do they offer their customers? Can you compete with their prices? Do you think their site is customer friendly? Could you give your customers something your competitors do not: more information, better deals, faster shipment, bonus gifts? Pay particular attention to promotion. Where do your competitors promote or advertise their site? Who are they trying to reach? How easy it is to find them? Are they offering other products in addition to the one you are interested in?

For a product or service to be sold successfully online, at least one of the following conditions must be met:

- **A great deal**. Your prices should undercut those of your competitors (at least your conventional competitors, such as neighborhood stores).

- **Availability.** Is your product difficult to find in stores? A product that's available only online or through mail-order sells better on the Internet. These products include unique items such as works of art and homemade crafts. In addition, some items are hard to get in certain countries: books published only in another nation, music CDs, clothing items, antiques, religious artifacts, etc. The Internet allows residents of one country to buy items directly from another even if they are not exposed to magazine or other media ads from that country.

- **Unparalleled customer service.** Let's assume that an online photo-supplies vendor sets up a site which offers information on photography and film developing, and displays samples of pictures taken with different types of film or under different lighting conditions. Photographers and photography buffs are going to return to such a site again and again. And as long as the prices are at least slightly less than those found at conventional stores (even if only for large quantities), many of these customers will purchase their supplies through this site. Why? Because people like to buy from professionals who know their business.

> What Internet users crave most of all is information. This can be in the form of text, photographs, audio recordings or video clips. It may sound like a cliché, but the average Internet user believes that the Internet is here to open a door to an unknown world, and to expand our horizon. This is the Internet mentality, and to succeed online you must pay its dues. Your site should not just sell items or services — it must give Internet users things that televison, radio and the print media cannot: abundant information; links to related sites (with more information); and quick, easy access to anything that has something to do with what you are selling. Oh, yes, they also appreciate interactivity (clicking on icons, sending their comments, etc.).

Types of Online Businesses

Almost all online businesses, whether they are part of a conventional business or Internet-only, fall under at least one of the following categories:

Retailers. These are the virtual shops, the online vendors. They may sell anything, from flowers to software. Buying from them is similar to ordering items from catalogs — the customer visits the site, selects an item, pays, and receives the product by mail. Most businesses of this category would also succeed as mail-order businesses — a detail that they all too often overlook.

Online businesses of other types often double as retailers. For instance, it would only be natural for an online travel agency to sell travel books, maps, and camping gear.

Businesses that sell custom-made/homemade products. Unlike most businesses of the first category, businesses that sell custom-made items take full advantage of what the Internet has to offer — namely, interactivity. One of the best examples of this type of business is a custom T-shirt printer. Customers select from a variety of graphic designs and shirt colors, and may even send (or upload) images of their own to be printed on the shirt.

Operating a business of this category has several advantages:

- **Ease of customer input.** The interactivity that goes hand in hand with this type of Internet business gives the customer instant gratification even before the ordered product arrives by mail.

- **The ability to be unique.** Customers can easily find T-shirts at their neighborhood clothing stores, but only at *your* Internet site can they find *your own* particular line of custom designs. Internet businesses of this category are not merely substitutes for conventional stores — they introduce original items or concepts to the market. This type of business can also market its products through conventional channels of distribution.

- **Small inventory.** Unlike most retailers, these businesses usually specialize in just one or two lines of products.

- **Less competition.** Businesses of this type are idea/talent-based. Since the items you sell are unique, you will have little to no competition. The profit margin for this type of business is therefore relatively high.

- **Creativity.** Operating one of these businesses is more interesting than operating a retail business. It offers a creative challenge, the opportunity to change and reinvent yourself as you go along, and the potential for coming up with "the idea of the decade" someday. It is certainly more fun than being a merchant or a middleman, and you will welcome every new working day with enthusiasm and vigor.

Bear in mind, however, that dealing with just one or two lines of product can make your business a little risky. For the beginner, it might be a good idea to tack on retail sales. For example, the above mentioned custom T-shirt site can also sell other clothing and related items which it will buy from a wholesaler.

Businesses that sell information. These businesses, too, take advantage of the Internet's interactivity. The customer browses through descriptions of several packages of information that are available on the site, and selects the package he wants. In most cases, once payment is settled, he can download the information (or receive it through e-mail) immediately, thus eliminating any delivery time. For example, let's assume that this customer wants to make his will. He visits a site that is dedicated to the subject, and from the menu selects the appropriate will package, which includes information and a few forms he can print out. The customer pays the site, then downloads the information package right away or requests that it be sent to him immediately via e-mail.

Advantages for the business operator:

- **No inventory whatsoever.**
- **No shipping and handling expenses.** Everything is transferred electronically. Sending a thousand information packages through e-mail costs the same as sending just one.

Brokerage and referral services also fall under this category. However, the information they give you is free. They make their money when there is an actual transaction (e.g., the customer pays a commission when purchasing a house).

Consulting services. These are online businesses with a human touch. Here, unlike any other category of Internet businesses, you will have to deal with your customers personally. For example, suppose that an amateur horticulturist finds out that his orchids are dying out due to an unknown reason. He contacts an online gardening center, and there he is put in touch with an expert, either through e-mail, a chat program, or even the telephone. The customer deals with a person, not an automated multi-media presentation (the site). The main drawback of this one-on-one approach is the inability to handle many customers in a short time. An Internet site of any other category can deal with hundreds of orders a day; an online consultant would have to hire more employees to be able to do that. On the plus side, an online consultant has no inventory or shipping expenses.

Businesses that sell services. Here, the final product is work performed for the consumer. Businesses of this type can be divided into two groups:

- **Conventional service companies with a presence on the Internet.** These businesses are mostly based in the conventional business world, and use their Internet site only as another means of promotion. Many of them have only local appeal. Examples: CPAs, computer repair services.

- **Online service companies.** With these businesses, no contact between the client and the server is necessary beyond that which the Internet provides (plus maybe a few phone calls). Such businesses include speech writers, editors and, of course, home page designers. The international potential of such businesses is almost unlimited.

Businesses that derive their income from advertising fees. The field of possibilities open for these businesses is vast. Anything goes — every idea, design or concept — as long as it pulls in the masses and records as many hits (visits to an online site) as possible. Such sites can offer information, entertainment, education, links to other sites, audio files, video files, free software and many other features. Businesses of this category have two things in common:

- **The main services they offer are *free*.**

- **They hope to attract as many visitors as possible to their site.** The more visitors they have, the higher the rate they can charge their advertisers. For accurate online traffic statistics, advertisers rely on independent Internet evaluation and measurement companies, such as I/PRO (http://quantum.ipro. com), which works together with Nielsen Media Research, or PC-Meter (http://www.npd.com). Don't expect advertisers to trust your site's own hit counter.

Some of the greatest online success stories fall under this category: Yahoo (http://www.yahoo.com) and other search engines; popular chat programs such as Freetel (http://www.freetel.com); news or magazine sites such as MSNBC (http://www.msnbc.com); and many others. Most, if not all, of their services are offered for free. Internet surfers would rarely agree to pay for entering a site, but even when you give them a free site that offers information or certain services at no charge, visitors can still make money for you so long as you sell advertising. Of all online business categories, this one seemed to have found the golden path between blending in with the Internet community and cashing in on it.

Of course, if you want a large number of people to visit your site, you will have to make it very interesting, or offer (for free) a service badly needed by Internet users. Expect to spend a lot more on promotion for this type of business than you would for any other.

When operating a business of this kind, keep the following in mind:

- **Don't make the ads on your site too large or conspicuous.** Visitors will understand and accept the fact that your site carries advertisements — this is the thing that allows them to enjoy your services free of charge. However, they want to see a site, not a billboard. Surf the Internet, and you will discover that most ads are confined to narrow bars on the top, side or bottom of Internet sites (these are called banner ads).

- **You may, of course, sell a few products or services** in addition to the free information or services you offer on your site. Do not forget, however, that this would be your *secondary* business. If your site is set up only to promote the products/services you sell, then this is not a free site, and the number of visitors will probably drop accordingly. The products or services you want to sell should be presented as just one option out of many on your site; one of several items in your main directory. They should not top the bill.

- **Although this is not a rule of thumb, any advertising you accept on your site should complement its subject matter.** If your site is a motorcycling center dedicated to bike maintenance, your visitors will probably welcome ads that sell bike accessories, and may even come to regard them as an important feature of your site. Not only will such ads not irritate the visitors to this site, they may even be counted in its favor. But it would be a totally different story were this professional motorcycling center to display ads for sex services.

    You may wonder why this point was brought up in the first place — it seems obvious that people should select ads that would complement their own site. And wouldn't the advertisers also be looking for such a correlation? In most cases this is the case, but not always. Surf the Internet, and you will be astonished at the number of irrelevant advertisements you will find there. Ads that promote get-rich-quick schemes or even legitimate services and products seem to be scattered all around the Net without any logic.

    Of course, the laws of supply and demand supersede all that is said here, and if one day you will find yourself having to choose between accepting irrelevant ads for display and going out of business, no one would expect you to choose the second option.

Internet sites that sell subscriptions. Here, the customer pays a monthly fee and receives a password that allows him to enter the Internet site. While there, he can view information, pictures, art, listen to audio files, etc. You should avoid this concept unless you are absolutely sure that the features on your site are so irresistible that people will be willing to pay just to enter it. Some online magazines as well as most adult entertainment sites fall under this category.

Promotional sites. The businesses of this category are a fusion between businesses who sell products or services (online or conventional) and free information sites. Promotional sites do not try to sell their items directly, but instead have the goal of educating consumers. Most large corporations maintain such sites, which display their products and allow the visitor access to information, pictures, or even technical support. Car manufacturers, for example, know that the chances of anyone buying a new car on the Internet are remote. However, they also know that displaying the features of new models online would help potential customers decide in favor of purchasing one of them. Since most small entrepreneurs do not have high-ticket items or products that are available in stores nationwide, this category is irrelevant to most of them.

For detailed information on specific businesses Internet entrepreneurs can establish, see *121 Internet Businesses You Can Start from Home* (Actium Publishing) by the author.

5

PROMOTION, ONLINE

Running a business on the Internet has many advantages for the entrepreneur, chief among them the low overhead. Most Internet businesses can be run from your own home. Even if you find along the way that you do have to rent a separate office or warehouse, you can choose the ones with the lowest rent, regardless of location (unless you need a retail outlet).

There is a catch, however. An Internet-based business owes its existence to just one thing — promotion. Even if a store owner does not promote or advertise his store, he can still rely on customers who walk in from the street. An Internet site that does not promote or advertise could never hope to attract any customers. It is that simple.

The object of this book is to show you that, with very few exceptions, the most effective promotion for an online business is not online but conventional, offline promotion. This does not mean that the Internet should be ignored as a medium for promoting your business. There *are* things you should do to promote your business online, and they will be discussed in this chapter.

The First Rule of Promotion:

Promote a great deal or a dream, not a product. There is little point in promoting a product or service if the promoter neglects to give customers an incentive to buy the item. If, for example, you sell batteries, and you promote your site as "The Battery Emporium," you might as well promote it as "A great place for finding the same old batteries for the same old prices." True, some people may be attracted to such a site (those who for some reason can't get batteries in their neighborhood store), but to get most people to visit your site, you would need a better promotion, which invariably means giving people a great deal.

What is a great deal? You might want to try: "Four batteries for the price of three"; "30% off every battery"; or "Free 9V battery with every $10 purchase." You may also want to remind your customers that you carry all batteries, including hard-to-get watch batteries.

The most important element of promotion is, therefore, having something other than a product to promote. This does not have to be a special deal. A dream is just as good. A dream is anything the customer wishes to have (or is convinced by the vendor that he wishes to have) and doesn't really need. Hanging a beautiful picture on his own living room wall can be a customer's dream. Participating in a new, exiting outdoors activity can be a dream. Owning a collection of yesteryear's top hits can be a dream. All these examples are products or services that customers do not really need, but want to have anyway. When you promote such items, your job is:

1. To remind the public that the items exist.

2. To let the public know that *you* have them.

Promoting "dream items" is harder than promoting "deal items," because no one is going to look for them. Nobody will look for an organizer of an outdoor activity he has never heard of. No one will look for a picture he has yet to see for the first time. When planning your promotion, it should be tailor-made to fit *one* of two concepts: either a good deal on items people need and are always looking for, or a tempting offer that people are not yet aware of and will not look for on their own. For example, registering your site with search engines (see ahead) would be a waste of time if no one is looking for the items you sell. This type of promotion does not fit "dream items."

How much should you spend on online promotion? Well, zero would be a good amount. Save your money for conventional promotion. Almost all ways of online promotion mentioned in this chapter do not cost money, which is by itself a good enough reason to take advantage of them.

Search Engines

The first thing you need to do once your Internet site is up and running is to register it with *search engines.* Internet users must use search engines to find sites. Without search engines, Net surfers would only have been able to visit sites whose addresses they had seen in ads, or those to which they link through other sites. Internet users can look up a site either by name (of a business or a person) or by subject. For example, keying in the word "stereo" will display links to all the sites that either deal with this subject, or simply mention the word. The user can narrow down the search by looking for "stereo+online+catalog," which would display stereo equipment stores with online catalogs.

These are the top search engines, and their URLs:

InfoSeek	http://www.infoseek.com/
Lycos	http://www.lycos.com/
Excite	http://www.excite.com/
Alta Vista	http://www.altavista.digital.com/
Yahoo	http://www.yahoo.com/
Hot Bot	http://www.hotbot.com/
Magellan	http://www.mckinley.com/
Web Crawler	http://www.webcrawler.com/
AOL Net Find	http://www.aol.com/netfind/

Hundreds of smaller search engines also exist on the Net, and you can reach most of them through *Go Net-Wide* at:

http://www.gonetwide.com/gopublic.html

> Some search engines (e.g., Yahoo) are directories as well as a search engines — you can search them as you would the Yellow Pages, not just by keywords.

You have to register your site with search engines yourself. Although many of the search engines regularly scour the Net for new sites, finding your Web site on their own might take them a very long time. Registering your site is a fairly simple process: on every search engine's home page, you will find a hypertext that says, "Add URL" or "Add your site." Click on this hypertext to be transferred to a special Web page that will ask you to submit your site's URL, e-mail address, and other relevant information such as land address or a short description of the site.

The search engine displays a link to your site (plus a short description) whenever someone is looking for it by its subject, name, or keywords. How does the search engine know how to classify your site? There are three ways:

- **It uses the information you have given it.** Some search engines ask you to include a short description of your site, your site's main subject, and a few keywords (for example, an online music store would use the keywords: music, band, lyrics, CD, album, etc).

- **It scans the site by itself**

- **It uses the site's *Meta file***

The last two items deserve a more elaborate explanation, since they are central to an effective placement of your site in a search engine's database.

Meta Files

A Meta file is a small text file that is attached to a Web document. It is not displayed to Internet users who visit your site, but search engines are able to read it. When designing a Web page, you can create Meta files to accommodate such information as title, author, description or keywords (every Web page authoring software allows this). Most search engines will display this data with the link they give your site. For example, let us assume that a business by the name of B&B Bargain Stationery writes a Meta file that describes its site's home page. The Meta file would look something like this:

```
<title> B&B Bargain Stationery</title>
<meta name="Author" content="John Smith">
<meta name="Description" content="Stationery: unbelievable
selection at unbelievable prices.">
<meta name="Keywords" content="envelopes,stationery,office,
supply,marker,paper,shipping,tape,pen,stickers,files,box,mailer,
labels, knife">
```

A search engine's link to this site will probably look like this to the user:

B&B Bargain Stationery
Stationery: unbelievable selection at unbelievable prices.

As you can see, only the site's title and description are displayed for the search engine user. The search engine does not display the keywords, but it uses them to help people find the site (i.e., if a person types the word "envelope" the search engine will display all the sites that have this word as a keyword or as part of their title or description).

Remember: every Web page has its own Meta file, not just the home page. Most search engines only require you to submit the home page of your site. The search engine then scans and classifies every page linked to this home page automatically. By using Meta files with individual Web pages, you can help the search engine classify them correctly. In the above example, if the home page contains a directory of the site (i.e., links to Web pages that are dedicated to envelopes, markers, copy machine cartridges, etc.), then each of the secondary Web pages should have its own Meta file with a short description of *its* own content.

> To view Meta files while surfing the Web, use the *View — Document Source* command on NetScape or *View — Source* on Microsoft Explorer. The Meta file information is displayed at the head of the document.

Evaluations by Search Engines

Many search engines do not trust Meta files, and prefer to scan all sites submitted to them themselves. The reason is that many online entrepreneurs have fallen into the habit of giving bogus information about their site. For example, imagine how a link to the site in the above example would look if, instead of the true description of the site, the Meta file's description were to read: "Rock & Roll CDs for free — you will never believe your eyes!" (Of course, such a tactic would surely backfire on the entrepreneur: it is highly unlikely that the thousands of users who will flock to the site because of the bogus description are interested in stationery. It is very likely, however, that they will be extremely angry with the entrepreneur, who will be bombarded with hate e-mail and who will lose potential customers.)

The search engine's concern is not for the damage this tactic would do to the entrepreneur, but for the damage it would do to itself. What use is a search engine if the information it displays is false? People who were not able to narrow down their searches (because irrelevant sites kept popping up under all search categories) would probably direct their anger at the search engine itself, and may stop using it altogether. The public places the responsibility for the accuracy of the information on the search engines, who therefore feel obligated to verify the information submitted to them by the sites they include in their database. They do this by scanning the site and analyzing its text content. Usually this is done automatically, by a special robot. The robot decides what keywords are to be used based on what it finds on the site. This may sometimes create problems, as many sites use catchy phrases and slogans instead of a succinct description of the site (and who can blame them?).

To avoid this problem, always include a few sentences that contain keywords within your Web pages, especially at the top of the document. A directory (which belongs on the home page, anyway) will also provide many keywords (a directory always mentions the subjects the site deals with).

Your link's position in the search results is very important. For example, search engine users who type in "travel agency" might be presented with several thousand links. Naturally, they will only visit the first 20 or 40 on the list. A travel agency appearing in the 200th place is, in the search engine's opinion, a lot less relevant to this search subject than those first 20 or 40. Very few search engine users will ever get to this link.

How do search engines gauge your site's relevancy to the subject it is supposed to deal with? The following criteria will help you improve your site's ranking with search engines:

- **The frequency of the subject word.** For example, let's assume that an Internet user is looking for all the sites that discuss Abraham Lincoln. When the search results appear, there may be thousands of sites that mention this subject. Those sites which mention Lincoln's name more than once (but not *too many* times! — see ahead), and include other related keywords, are probably going to appear at the top of the list.

- **Keywords in the title.** Search engines assume that a site is more relevant to a search subject if the subject words appear in the title. A Web page with the title "The Abraham Lincoln Fact Sheet" is probably more relevant to users who search for "Abraham Lincoln" than a Web page entitled "Political Assassinations," although the latter may also include information on Abraham

Lincoln. Remember that every Web page has its own title. If you have not created a title for a Web page (Web authoring software allow you to do this when you create a Meta file), the search engine will consider the first sentence it reads as its title. To be on the safe side, make sure the first sentence on your home page *is* the title. Reserve catchy phrases and commercial hooks for the second or third sentence.

- **The position of keywords on your Web page.** If most of the keywords appear at the top of your page, most search engines will assume that your site is dedicated to the keyword's subject.

- **How many sites link to your page** (not how many sites *your page* links to). The more popular your site is, the higher search engines will judge its relevancy to the subject it deals with. Not every search engine regards this as a criterion, but having many links to your site will improve your relevancy ranking with at least some of them.

- **Search engines hate frames.** *Frames* are the windows or split screens many Web sites use nowadays. Normally, one window contains the site's directory, and the other its content. The directory window stays in its place even when you link to another page (within the same site). Sometimes a third window is also found with a chat program, the site's e-mail address, or commercial ads. Although frames make a site look interesting, most search engines cannot penetrate them and therefore do not classify them correctly. The solution is either:

  1. **Don't use frames.** You can achieve the same effect by duplicating the directory/ads and posting them on every Web page of your site.

  2. **Set up a mirror site,** which will not use frames, but will be able to link visitors to your "framed" site.

- **Be aware that there are some keywords that most search engines ignore.** These include words so common almost every site uses them, such as "Web" or "Site." It is better not to rely on these as keywords.

- **If your site is reviewed by a person rather than a robot, then that person's decision supersedes any robot decision.** If you believe that your site was unfairly treated (for example, it is found in the 200th position under the search word that is its main subject), you can contact the search engine by e-mail or land mail and ask that an employee reviews it. There are many sites that deal exclusively with one subject matter and yet are very hard to find under this subject because they do not contain enough keywords, or use graphics instead of text.

- **There are search engines that are harder to submit sites to than others.** Such search engines take a long time to register new sites or update existing ones. Sometimes new sites are not added to their database at all. If you encounter such problems, your best bet is to send the non-responsive search engine an e-mail message (or a letter) telling them how long you have been waiting and asking them to expedite their indexing. On the bright side, there are search engines such as InfoSeek, which normally take only minutes to add your site to their database.

Search Engines and Spam

Search engines do not look kindly on *spam*. Spam is a widely used term for unsolicited commercial messages, or unethical promotional tactics online. Here are a few of these tactics, which some online businesses have used to get a better position for their sites with search engines:

- **Invisible ink.** If your site's background is white, and you use white-colored text, this text will not be seen by visitors, but search engines' robots will be able to read it. Some entrepreneurs use such invisible texts to convey messages or add keywords that are not relevant to the site's subject.

- **Duplicating keywords.** Some entrepreneurs operate under the assumption that repeating a keyword ten and sometimes even a hundred times will place their site in a higher position in the search engine's database. Often these entrepreneurs use invisible ink to duplicate these keywords so that visitors will not notice them. The keywords are usually added to the bottom of the Web page, where they don't take useful space. Many search engines have special filters to prevent repetitive keywords from determining the site's relevancy.

- **Using irrelevant keywords.**

- **Registering the same Web page under different titles or descriptions.** This can have the same effect as using irrelevant keywords, because people would find the same page under a variety of subjects, some of them not related to its topic.

When a search engine encounters a case of spam, its reaction will range from not accepting this particular Web page to striking all of the site's pages (which appear under the same domain name) off its databases. The punishment may be permanent or temporary, but it is always very inconvenient for the entrepreneur. Should this happen to you, and you feel that you did not try to use irrelevant keywords or descriptions, contact the search engine, explain your case, and ask that a *person* reviews your site.

Updating

Search engines constantly update their databases, and may scan your site more than once. If, for example, your virtual beeper store appears in the 10th place when a user searches for the keyword "beeper" (which is a very good position), don't be surprised if just a week later it slips to the 15th place, a month later to the 50th, and after two more months to the 600th (which is as good as nonexistent). You have to register and re-register your site (at least the home page) on a regular basis if you want search engine users to find you. You may also want to examine the sites that are ahead of you in line. Are they more relevant to the search subject than yours? Do they, for example, offer more information about beepers? Better phrased sentences that convey the message more accurately than yours?

If all you want out of a search engine is that it would help users find your site by name only (not by subject), don't bother with constant updating. When your specific business name is keyed in, your site is probably going to be the only one or one of a few to appear— even if it is found in the $200,000^{th}$ place when searched by subject.

If you do not have the time to submit your site to search engines yourself, there are many services that would do it for you. Keep in mind, however, that most of these services will probably do a worse job at it than you. Many search engines require you to type in a short description of your site, your company, etc. — make sure the site submitting service does this for you. Some site submitting services will guarantee your site a top position on the search engines' list. Ask them if they can also guarantee that your site will stay at that position for more than a couple of days.

An excellent tool for checking on your site's position in search engines is Position Agent (http://www.positionagent.com). In addition to their paid services, they offer free access to a special software that checks your site's position in the most popular search engines. All you have to do is enter your site's URL and the keyword it should be searched under, and the results appear on your screen in a few seconds.

Figure 5-1 A sample of a Web site that would not rank high with search engines.

A.T.D. BARGAIN WAREHOUSE

Blowout

 Sale!!

Guaranteed low prices on all your photographic needs!

WE WILL MEET OR BEAT ANY PRICE!

HUGE QUANTITY DISCOUNTS!

SAVE $$$ THE NEXT TIME YOU TAKE A VACATION

For our summer discount price list, click on icons.

<u>Free Tips</u>

Figure 5-2 The same Web site after a few changes: Search engines will consider this page much more relevant to the subject of photography/film

---

A.T.D. PHOTO WAREHOUSE

All your photographic needs: point & shoot cameras, 35mm film (color, black & white, slides) 110 film, disposable cameras, filters.

Blowout

Sale!!

Guaranteed low prices on:

<u>Film</u> Kodak, Fuji, Konica, Polaroid, 3M

<u>Cameras</u> Point & shoot, disposable, panoramic

<u>Most other</u> photographic supplies

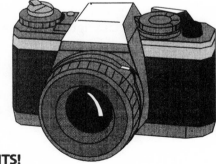

WE WILL MEET OR BEAT ANY PRICE!

HUGE QUANTITY DISCOUNTS!

SAVE $$$ ON FILM THE NEXT TIME YOU TAKE A VACATION

For our summer discount price list, click on icons or hypertext.

<u>Free Tips: How to take great pictures with your camera</u>

Search Engines — A Realistic View

Do not place too much importance on search engines. Some of the most successful sites cannot be found in the first 20 or 30 pages of the search results if you look for them by subject (search results usually appear 10-20 to a page). Monitoring and re-submitting your site to search engines may take many hours of your time every week, and with the increasing competition for good positions your site may never be in one of the top positions after all (especially if you deal with a popular subject such as books, beepers, etc.). It is probably wiser to direct your effort and energy to other methods of promotion. Of course, if your site's subject is narrow (e.g., your site deals with the works of one artist), search engines can do wonders for you.

You can try to narrow down your site's subject even if you do work with popular items. For instance, if you sell software, your site would probably never appear in one of the top positions under this subject. Try instead to concentrate on a smaller niche. A combination of the keywords "software" and "first aid" would yield far fewer search results than the keyword "software" alone. If you concentrate on this type of software, you stand a much better chance of being found, because anyone searching with the keywords "software first aid" will see your site *before* larger, unspecialized software stores.

Lastly, if you don't want your site to be indexed, scanned or included in search engines' databases, you can either remove it from them or exclude your site to begin with by entering a special "noindex" command in your Meta file. Of course, very few commercial sites have been known to do this.

Links

Links should not be underestimated as means of promotion. Internet surfers use links regularly while navigating the Net. You can get other sites to place links to your site in one of the following ways:

- **By convincing them that your site deals with a subject which their visitors will find interesting.** You would have an even better case if your site complements the other site. For example, an online travel agency would benefit from displaying a link to a site that takes car rental reservations online. This adds resources to the first site, and improves its customer service.

- **By offering to place a reciprocal link to their site.** This link exchange strategy is really advertising in disguise, where the advertiser pays the site with ad space. Keep in mind, however, that while some sites welcome such a barter, others are only interested in links to relevant sites that would be of interest to their visitors. When approaching the latter, it's best to say that you have placed a link to their site, and that you hope they will find your site of interest to their visitors. Don't make it sound like a threat: "Please link to my site or I'll pull the link I placed to yours" would make a very poor impression on anyone.

- **By using an agent.** An agent will place links to your site in various other sites (which may or may not require reciprocal links) for a certain fee. These link services can probably place many more links than you can. The drawback is that many of these links may appear in irrelevant sites. For example, if you sell boat accessories online, your chances of getting many visitors from a linked wedding gown shop are remote. For a list of link services, either type "link" in any one of the search engines, or go to:

http://www.realitycom.com/bamboo/submit.html-ssi

- **By paying them.** If you take this step, you can expect your link to be more than just an underlined URL with a short description. This, of course, can be regarded as advertising (see Chapter 7 for more details).

Naturally, it is also a good idea to place links from your site to other sites, including those who do not reciprocate. This will add resources to your own and in essence enlarge your site. You can concentrate all links on a special "links page" and include it as an item in your site's main directory. Many Internet users look for link pages. Make sure the sites you link to are relevant to your site's subject matter.

What's New

There is a story of a man who kept complaining about his car, but when he finally managed to sell it, he purchased a new car of the same model. "Why?" his friends asked him. "You've always said it was a lousy automobile!" "Yes," he said, "but this year they came out with a totally redesigned model — it has a new dashboard!"

You would have to scour the Internet for hours before you'll find a site that offers something that's *truly* new and innovative — a new product, a new technology, a completely new service — and yet, self proclamations of "newness" are as abundant as new commercial sites. Most new sites don't have anything new to offer, but the fact that they themselves are new is often enough to attract visitors. The Internet users' mentality is somewhat similar to that of the man in the story — they regard every old thing with a new twist and a Web site as new. The reasons for this are unclear. Perhaps it is the fact that everything about the Internet is new — from the Internet itself, to the ever-upgraded computer hardware Internet users own. Maybe it is the unending coverage the Internet gets from the news media. Whatever the reason, the fact is net surfers expect to discover something new behind every corner. Entrepreneurs should take heed of this mentality, and take advantage of it.

What's-New services are directories that list new sites on the Internet. Many search engines and directories have a What's New page (e.g., Yahoo), and these are very popular with Internet users. As their name suggests, What's New directories only list the new sites for a short time (2-4 weeks). Still, if you manage to get your site mentioned by one of the popular directories, you can expect to receive tens of thousands of visitors during those few weeks. If only a fraction of these will become repeat visitors, you will have created a significant customer base right from the start.

Assuming that you did not come up with a revolutionary new product or service, your problem is probably going to be how to convince What's New directories that your site is worth including in their list. You can do this in two ways:

- **By tying your site with popular themes, trends or fashion.** Let's suppose, for example, that the top issue on the nation's agenda is protecting the public against biological warfare, and that this problem is repeatedly discussed and debated by the media. If you sell books on your site, you may want to dedicate a few pages to this issue, and offer site visitors books on the subject, links to relevant sites, audio clips of experts discussing the issue (with their permission, of course), information, survival tips and more. Some who drop by will come for this subject, and stay around to browse books on other topics.

- **By giving an existing product/service a new angle or twist.** For example, if you sell sunglasses, your site can feature a 3-D head wearing the sunglasses the customer selects. Customers will be able to see how the sunglasses they have picked look on a "real person," and can then either purchase them or make another selection. There's nothing new about the product in this example, but the convenient online feature may endear your site to the hearts of the What's New directories.

If you cannot manage to get your site included in the top What's New directories, do not despair. First, very few small new sites make it to those directories, and secondly, there are many other What's New directories, which are smaller and more accessible. Here are three of them (for a full list use the keywords, "What's New" or "Whats New" with any of the search engines):

- ▸ **Webcrawler's What's New**
  http://webcrawler.com/select/nunu.new.html (Choose "Add URL" to include your site)

▸ **What's New on the Internet**
http://www.emap.com/whatsnew/addyours.shtml

▸ **What's New Too**
http://newtoo.manifest.com/WhatsNewToo/submit.html
(This site promises to post your listing within 36 hours)

Newsgroups

Newsgroup promotion seems so inexpensive, easy and efficient, it is easy to forget that it can also backfire on you. A commercial message posted to a newsgroup is spam — unsolicited, unwanted electronic junk mail. True — some people may read your message and visit your site, but most newsgroup subscribers will be angry at your commercial message and would never do business with you. In addition, a few extremists among them might:

- **Flame you.** In other words, e-mail bomb you with hundreds of *hate e-mail* messages. Even if you use a false e-mail address for your newsgroup posting (which is illegal), people can still find out your real e-mail address by visiting your site or contacting your server. Angry subscribers who cannot find your e-mail address might send hate mail to your land address instead — after all, you would have to display some contact information on your site, such as e-mail or land mail addresses or a telephone/fax number.

- **Use the same newsgroups to defame you.** For example, angry subscribers might follow each of your commercial postings with a false complaint about your business, products, quality of service, etc.

Some newsgroups (particularly those that deal with entrepreneurship and home business) have been taken over completely by commercial messages. Anyone clicking on one of these newsgroups is overwhelmed by several thousands of spam messages, while legitimate messages (discussions and questions) are almost nonexistent. To add insult to injury, many spammers often post their messages in batches of ten or twenty to stand out from the crowd. This only causes the newsgroup to swell in size, and makes viewing them a tedious and boring affair. In such newsgroups (who have already lost the war to commercial ads), subscribers see little point in taking steps against spammers. Keep in mind, however, that any commercial ads you post to them will be lost among thousand of others in a newsgroup that very few people bother to take seriously and read anymore.

How, then, should you use newsgroups for effective promotion? The key word here is *Netiquette.* Don't impose on newsgroups — serve them. For example, let us suppose that an entrepreneur is running a search service for rare automobile parts. The following message, even if posted only to relevant newsgroups, would be considered spam:

> Looking for that hard-to-get part? Search no further! Visit our site at http://www.... From a 1912 Ford T to exotic limited-production sports cars, we'll search and FIND all the engine or body parts you need — original or remanufactured.

The message below is so transparent, it is even worse than the first one:

> I've heard of a great place for rare automobile parts. Their URL is http://www.... They can find anything, and for the right price!

Instead of posting unsolicited messages, this entrepreneur should read legitimate newsgroup messages and respond to them. For example, let's take a question that was posted to a newsgroup dedicated to auto repairs:

> I've searched high and low for a water pump for a' 77 Landrover but no dice. Please help!

In response, it is perfectly alright for the entrepreneur to reply:

I think http://www......... can get it.

Short, succinct and helpful, this message would not alienate potential customers. Also, the subscriber who had asked the question would not be the only one to read the reply. In newsgroups that deal with automobiles, many other participants will be interested in a good source for rare parts. Since the above reply does not reek of commercialism, its effect would be as good as that of a recommendation from a friend.

Since newsgroup messages stay posted for at least two to three days before they expire, it is enough to check relevant newsgroups only twice or three times a week for leads. Unlike chat programs, newsgroups are not a real-time communication tool, and you will not miss important questions.

What happens if there are no questions for you to answer? Some entrepreneurs become creative, getting a friend to post questions for them, or even posting them themselves. Bear in mind, though, that service providers forbid users from posting messages under a false name or misleading e-mail address (although this happens all the time). They usually take action against the violators (from a warning to cancellation of the account) only when someone complains to them about spam messages.

There are thousand of newsgroups, and their number is increasing steadily. You have to select only the newsgroups that are relevant to your business, or your promotional efforts will be wasted. Don't try to browse through all of them to find the few relevant ones — this would take days. Instead, go to:

http://www.dejanews.com

DejaNews is a search engine for newsgroups. Just type in a keyword, and DejaNews will display all the messages posted during the course of the past few weeks that mention this keyword, and the names of the newsgroups they were posted to. For example, if you sell car covers online, and are looking for the right newsgroups to monitor, keying in the word "auto" will display all the newsgroups that deal with cars or the auto industry, such as: rec.autos.driving; misc.transport.urban-transit; rec.autos.marketplace.

You can also start your own newsgroup, but chances are that few people would visit it. Keeping a newsgroup interesting and building a loyal reader-base is very hard work.

Direct E-mail

Known as the scourge of the Internet, you would not score too many points with potential customers by using this method. Direct e-mail simply involves sending massive quantities of unsolicited commercial messages to Internet users. A special software sends the thousands (and sometimes millions) of e-mail messages automatically according to a mailing list purchased from certain list brokers. The list can be general (everyone with an e-mail address) or limited to certain groups (e.g., people who have bought software online during the past two years).

The cost of sending these unsolicited messages is minimal, and so, unlike the conventional junk mail we receive through our mail box, e-mail junk can haunt us for years with little reason for the sender to stop. The result? Internet users are bombarded daily with unsolicited messages which take time to download and delete. Some Internet users have to deal with no less than 20 or 30 such messages daily, and waste a good ten minutes of their time waiting for them to download, sifting through them to find real messages from friends and business associates, and deleting them. The longer an Internet user has been online, the greater are the chances of her e-mail address falling into the hands of mailing list compilers, and the more messages she will receive.

Where do the mailing list compilers get their e-mail addresses?

- **They buy them from online vendors.** Customers who buy from online vendors are often asked for their e-mail address. Many companies ask for your permission to pass this information on to a third party, but not all.

- **They scan newsgroup postings.** Just post a message (with your e-mail address) to a newsgroup that deals with home business, for example, and you are guaranteed to begin receiving unsolicited messages within days, if not hours.

Often spammers use devious tricks to get your attention when sending unsolicited messages. Instead of a subject line that describes their business or product, you will see something such as: "Hi, haven't heard from you in a long time." Of course, when you open the message, you discover that its content has nothing to do with the bogus subject line. This only serves to prolong the process of sorting out incoming e-mail messages, and further aggravates the user.

Most if not all Internet users hate unsolicited messages, and hence the company that sends them. Virtually all the Internet users the author knows swear that they will never buy from these companies, even if their product is cheaper than that of all their competitors. Some Internet users respond by flaming the spammers — sending them hate e-mail (or hate land-mail). Most of the spammers are new, fledgling companies, and many are viewed by Internet users as con artists.

It is best that you do not promote your business this way. You may find that you are making far more enemies for yourself than customers. Of course, if your customers have requested that you send them information through e-mail, this would not be considered spam.

Laws are now proposed with the aim of putting a stop to unsolicited direct e-mail. For details on current legislation, visit:

http://www.cauce.org

As with other means of promotion, the important thing to remember is that to be successful on the Internet, you have to respect Internet mentality and etiquette. Never alienate your potential customers.

Online Malls

Online malls (see page 39) can be used for promoting your Web site even if you have not set up your site with them. Some of them double as directories, and allow businesses to list their name and a short description for free. For a directory of about 500 malls (not all offering this free service), visit:

http://nsns.com/MouseTracks/HallofMalls.html

On-Site Promotion

Why would you want to use your own site for promotion? After all, only people who have already found it will be exposed to this promotion!

This is invariably true, but on-site promotion can serve two important purposes:

- **It creates repeat visitors.**

- **It encourages word-of-mouth promotion** — and many people believe this to be the best kind of all. Instead of forgetting about your site the minute they leave it, visitors who are exposed to on-site promotion might tell their friends and family about it.

Here are a few ideas for on-site promotion:

- **Sweepstakes.** This proven tactic can work just as well online as it does through mail-order. As a merchant, the best prize you can offer customers/visitors is your own product. You can allow your visitors to participate anonymously, but the best online business approach is to request that they enter their personal information and any comments they might have. By doing this, you will have gained three advantages:

1. The visitor interacts with your business rather than remaining a mute observer.

2. You can compile a list of potential customers' e-mail addresses. To encourage visitors to participate, post a written guaranty reassuring them that their personal information will not be forwarded to third parties and mailing list brokers. Don't forget to ask for permission to send them e-mail messages (such as news updates or product information).

3. You will gather demographic information that will help you (and advertisers) better understand who your customers are.

- **Quizzes.** These are similar to sweepstakes, with the exception that the customer has to show a certain degree of knowledge in your area of business or line of products in order to qualify for a prize. The customer, therefore, is made to take an interest in your business. You don't want to make the questions too hard, or visitors to your site will be turned off. The quiz should be of a general nature. For example, the Internet site of a film vendor can present its visitors with questions about black and white photography techniques. People like to put their knowledge of general subjects or trivia to the test, but would not bother to learn about a particular firm.

- **Contests.** Unlike a quiz, participants in a contest have to do something better than everyone else. Many visitors may answer a quiz correctly, but with a contest there is but one winner, one prize to give away (and maybe smaller second and third prizes). The contest, of course, should be related to your business. The film vendor in the above example can hold a best-landscape-photograph contest, and offer a lifetime supply of film as first prize.

- **A constantly changing feature.** For example, the film vendor can display a Photo-of-the-Day in his Web site. Amateur photographers might drop in from time to time just to watch this changing exhibition. Another possible feature is free software that visitors to your site could download (freeware). For example: demo versions of computer games; applications that enable users to hear audio recordings; etc.

- **Links.** To use the above example once more, the film vendor's site can make itself "The first place on the Internet a shutterbug would want to visit" by linking to many similar and related sites. In other words, you can turn your site into a mini-Web-directory, dedicated to just one subject.

All the above features are designed to keep visitors coming back to your site and to make them want to tell their friends about it. On-site promotion will certainly help your business, but keep in mind that it requires constant maintenance and updating, and may greatly increase the amount of time you have to devote to your site. Check the local authorities for laws and regulations governing sweepstakes and contests in your state.

Hitchhiking

Let's suppose that a new fad is sweeping the nation, or perhaps a new movie has come out, or a controversial news items becomes the talk of the town. Suppose you have the walk-through instructions to a new computer game, or an interesting commentary on a sports event, or a rare interview with a celebrity. Suppose, in a nut shell, that you have an idea that is bound to attract masses of visitors to your Internet site, but which has nothing to do with your line of business. How can you harness the pulling power of a "hot site" to your regular business site? In theory, you can combine both. However, you are running the risk of alienating both your customers (who will consider your site less professional if completely irrelevant material is found there) and the visitors who come to see the hot site.

What you should do is build the hot site as a separate, completely independent site that cannot be reached from your business site, but with the following hypertext link added to it:

"Thanks to [your business name and URL] for hosting this site"

Any visitors to the hot site who are interested in visiting your business site will be able to do so with ease. You can also add a logo or a second line describing the business site, but don't make it too long.

How many of the visitors to the hot site will visit your business site? Probably not too many. Entrepreneurs who have tried this promotional tactic talk of numbers in the range of .1%-1%. One tenth of a percent does not sound like much, but bear in mind that a hot site can pull in a huge number of hits. Many hot sites record 50,000-100,000 hits daily.

There are three problems with hot sites:

- **Their popularity is usually temporary.** For example, let's suppose that a famous movie star passes away. During the first days, and perhaps weeks, after the death, the public would be starved for any piece of information, gossip or pictures of that person. An ad-hoc site that provides this material will no doubt attract many visitors during that period. However, interest in the celebrity will wane in the months that follow, and the site will cease to be a hot site.

- **They can be costly.** Sites that attract tens of thousands of hits per day require high-speed server equipment that can handle this volume of traffic. This may cost you a few hundred dollars extra per month. Check with your server service before you open a high-traffic site.

- **They can be a hassle.** Sites that attract tens of thousands or hundreds of thousands of people daily might yield hundreds of e-mail messages per day — requests, questions, comments, suggestions. Answering these on a regular basis might turn out to be a full-time job. One way around this is to post the most popular questions in a FAQ (Frequently Asked Questions) Page that visitors can read before sending you e-mail. Another way is to apologize for not being able to answer every e-mail in person and let your auto responder send them all a form reply.

Choosing What Is Right for Your Business

Not every promotional method mentioned in this chapter (as well as the next) is right for your business. Some companies may find that while search engines work very well for them, What's New services or newsgroups are not much help. Others may reach the opposite conclusion. It will take time to figure out what works for you and what doesn't. Don't feel guilty if you cannot use every promotional method described in this book. Stick to the strategies and features that serve your business the best.

6

PROMOTION, CONVENTIONAL

Should you one day decide to throw away this book, do yourself a favor first: tear out and save this chapter. Conventional, offline promotion is the most important aspect of running your business (whether it's online, conventional or combined). This is the thing you want to put your best efforts into, and devote most of your time to. Reasons? To begin with, not all your customers will be able to reach you online. As we have discussed in earlier chapters, your best bet is not to open a strictly online business, but a combined online-offline one. Many of your customers may not have an Internet connection and any online promotion would be lost on them.

Also, conventional media is far more popular than the Internet. Many more people read the newspaper, listen to the radio, or watch TV than log onto the Internet. We also have to remember that Internet users are exposed to other media, too. It is common for new Internet subscribers to lose interest in conventional media for their first few months of Net surfing, but most make a full recovery in a relatively short time.

For a promotional campaign to strike the right note, you must first ask yourself what media your potential customers prefer. For instance, if you sell camping gear, your likely buyers may look for you under the subject words, "camping gear," in search engines. However, these same people, and many other potential customers who do not have Internet access, also read magazines dedicated to camping, nature, fishing, sports or travel. They also read related columns in general newspapers and watch television shows that deal with the same subjects.

As an entrepreneur, your best bet would be to spend most of your promotional budget on the above conventional media and on other promotional methods described in this chapter. Remember that **promotion is not the same as advertising**. When you advertise your business, you buy the space or time to tell potential customers about it; when you promote, you influence *other people* to tell potential customers about it (without paying them).

Press/News Releases

Since this is probably the most cost-effective means of promotion for all businesses great and small, you should invest much of your time mastering and perfecting this method. The first thing to remember about press releases (when sent to any media other than newspapers they are called *news releases*), is that they are not letters to the media. A press release is mock news coverage of your business or product as you think it should appear in the media. When you send a press release to a magazine, you are communicating with that magazine's readers, not its editors.

Press releases save the editor time. Instead of writing about your business or products, all she needs to do is edit your release and print it. The finished text, usually trimmed to fit the printing needs of the publication, appears as a news item — not an ad nor a letter to the newspaper.

Since press releases are not ads and they appear as news items, they have more impact on readers than ads. Less than 20% of people believe a commercial ad, but a news item is likely to be trusted by at least three times as many readers. Also, people take the time to read a news items, while most ads are ignored regardless of their size or color scheme. A good press release often achieves the effect that ten full-page ads would never have. And it's free!

Editors like press releases because they save them time while providing newsworthy material to add to their publication.

Entrepreneurs like press releases because they generate free publicity (save mailing expenses). However, for every press release that gets published, dozens end up in the waste basket. As a business promoter, you have to convince the editor that your press release is:

A. Up to standard.

B. Newsworthy.

The Presentation of Your Release

When they first take your press release out of the envelope, the editors will look at the document itself. Before the first sentence is read, and regardless of its content, your press release will be judged by how close it comes to the media's accepted standards. These are the technical requirements you must adhere to when writing your press release:

- **The document must be either typed on a typewriter or printed on an ink-jet or laser printer.** Some of the 24 pin dot matrix printers will also do nicely, but a 9 pin printer is not up to the task. Its printout is hard to read and makes a terrible first impression.

- **The text must be double-spaced.** Editors use this space to mark their corrections or write notes. If you are using a word processor, chances are you can set the line spacing in tenths (e.g., 1.8, 1.7). Use this feature if you need to fit more lines on a page.

- **Margins:** leave at least 1" on both sides and on the bottom. This space is also reserved for editors' notes. Your letterhead design usually determines your top margin.

- **Length:** one page is best, two are tolerable, three — unacceptable. Editors do not print lengthy press releases in their publications anyway, so a long release means more editing and cutting work for them.

- **No staples.** The pages should either be loose or attached to each other with a paper clip.

- **Use 8½" x 11" or legal size paper.** The latter has the advantage of allowing you to fit more double-spaced text on one page. It also requires a larger envelope, which would stick out from most of the other envelopes on the editor's desk and therefore command attention.

- **A header** should be printed at the top of the release, with contact information. You should include such items as your company name, telephone number, address, e-mail, etc. A contact name should appear at the upper right-hand side of the release. If you have two pages, be sure to include identifying and contact information on the second page as well, since pages are often misplaced in a busy editor's office.

- **A release date** must be included at the head of the document. The *release date* indicates the date before which the press release is not to be published. This is useful for business owners who want the publication of their press release to coincide with other promotion. If you have no need for a delay in publication, simply write: "For Immediate Release."

- **A Kill date** must also appear on the top of the document. A *kill date* is the last date the release can be used (e.g., when a special sale ends). Writing "No kill date" indicates that you set no time limits on the publication of your press release.

- **Three asterisks** (* * *) or the newspaper termination sign (*-30-*) should appear at the end of the release copy. Although this is not an immutable law, it will indicate to the editor that the writer of the release is a professional. These marks separate the content of the press release from your contact information or any notes to the editor you might want to add.

- **The pages on which the press release is written must be clean of smudges and stains.** If you use a copy machine, make sure it does not leave marks on the pages, and that the text is not blurry. Editors consider unclean, unclear copies to be sent by amateurs, and they tend to be the first to be balled up and pitched into the waste basket.

- **Proofread your copy.** Look for typos, misspelled words and grammar mistakes. In general, you want to avoid anything that reeks of amateurism.

- **Many editors appreciate it when you submit your press release on a floppy disk**, since it saves them a lot of retyping time. You can either include a disk with your press release or let the editor know one is available (e.g., by writing: "To receive the contents of this press release on disk, send an e-mail message to ... or call ....). You can also give the editor the option of receiving this text file via e-mail. **Never send a disk without a hard copy of the press release.** Editors are busy people, and they will not take the time to open and read the files on your disk if they are not sure they want to use it in their publication.

- **Press releases should best be sent through land mail, not e-mail.** Hard copies seem more professional and are taken more seriously.

Writing Your Press Release

Now, you must sit down and write the press release itself — your message to the people (not to the editor!). The best approach, which will greatly improve your press release's chances of getting published, is to put yourself in the editor's place. You are running a newspaper or a magazine. You are looking for newsworthy articles to print. These articles have to be interesting, relevant to the periodical's subject matter, new, and professionally written so that they will not reflect poorly on your publication. The one thing you are *not* looking for is giving businesses free ad space. For this reason, you will not pick the press releases that are too self serving or that look like a sales letter. Since the press release is printed in your periodical as *your* article, any claims made in it would be deemed to be coming from you. You cannot print sentences such as "The best prices in New York" since this would imply that you endorse this statement.

To be interesting, a press release must tell a story. Perhaps there is a new Web site that may be of interest to the periodical's readers. Maybe there is a new online service that will make life easier for people who want to find a reliable baby-sitter for their children. As an editor, you would ask yourself two questions:

1. Will this article help my readers?

2. Is the article written in an interesting way?

You don't have to be a Steinbeck or a Hemingway to write an interesting article. Simply keep in mind the "you" approach: write as you would like others to write for you (as a magazine reader). The following tips might help:

- **If you capture your reader's attention within the first two or three sentences, half the battle is won.** Start your release with an interesting, odd or provocative question ("How often do you donate money to your neighborhood car thief?"), quote ("It takes me five minutes to find a car to steal, five minutes to break into it, and the rest of the day to wonder at the average car owner's stupidity"), or statistics ("New survey shows over 50% of car owners had their car stolen at least once"). Naturally, all the above examples can serve as an opening line for the press release of an auto security-systems manufacturer.

- **Once you grab your readers' attention, give them information, not a sales copy.** Write a story of sorts. A short mock interview with a professional, a customer, the business owner, or anyone that can "move the plot" is a good way to start. In the above example, right after the opening sentence, an interview with a car thief can illuminate a few of the more common oversights of car owners. The interview can include tips on parking your car in a safe place, making it less attractive to car thieves etc.

- **Now it's time to mention your business or product.** Use sentences such as: "Car owners can find many more tips on preventing their vehicle from being stolen at http://www........ The new site, which was set up by ABCDE Auto Security, also offers consultation services and a virtual store for steering wheel locks."

- **Don't toot your own horn.** Jingles, catchphrases, and any attempt at self-praise will never make it past the editor. You may, however, use quotes from other people (e.g., customers or experts) who talk about your Web site or product. Again — make sure your press release does not look like a commercial ad.

- **Don't write your press release as you would a suspense story.** The most important things you want to say to the reader should appear in the first half of the release. One reason for this is that many, if not most people never read an article all the way to the end. The second reason is that editors tend to cut from the bottom should they need to trim your press release.

- **Your contact information** should appear at the bottom of the release' copy (address, phone number, e-mail, but not the Web site's URL — this must appear in the body of the text). Editors will not always print this information, but it's worth trying.

- **Use short sentences.** The average reader's already short attention span is further reduced by complex sentences or big words.

- **If possible, hitch a ride on current trends, fads, events, news items and anything of popular appeal.** Of course, you would have to find a veritable link between the above items and the topic of your press release, but you stand a better chance of getting it published if you do. It should not be too obvious that you are taking advantage of a topical subject to promote your business. Avoid spurious, labored attempts such as: "But most of the people who attended last week's Saint Patrick's day parade probably did not realize that during those three hours 1,020 people died due to tobacco smoking related illnesses. Had they only visited the Quit Smoking Center on http://www........"

- **Remember that editors will cut out at least some of your press release.** They will, of course, cut the least important parts, so make sure these parts do not contain important information. Try to concentrate the most important information in one or two paragraphs so that these paragraphs will not be cut.

- **A recurring theme in well-written press releases is the *problem and solution*.** The press release describes a problem, and presents your business, Internet site or product as the solution.

Press releases should be sent to three types of media:

- **To the trade/industry.** For example, if you sell exercise equipment, health and fitness magazines may want to hear from you, as well as radio/ TV shows and online services that deal with this subject. You should also address your press releases to newsletters of health and fitness organizations and associations.

- **To local media.** Local media outlets may take an interest in you simply because you are located in the neighborhood or city they cover. They love to report on the region's entrepreneurs, even if their business has a presence only on the Internet.

- **To everyone else.** If your press release appears in one of the high-circulation periodicals, you are looking at tens of thousands of visits to your site. Even newspapers with a circulation of 100,000 can do much for you. Naturally, the higher the circulation, the smaller your chances of seeing your press release in print, so newspapers or magazines with a circulation of less than 100,000 should not be overlooked. If you think your site or product appeals to young adults, you may also want to try college and school newsletters, who normally receive only a handful of press releases every month, and who will therefore be more likely to publish your release.

Perhaps the most important thing to remember about press releases is this: quantity has a quality of its own. Even if your press release is one of the best ever written, there is still the element of chance to consider. Editors, especially of high-circulation periodicals, receive many more press releases than they can handle. Even after weeding out the badly written or self-serving ones, the editor is sometimes left with 20 or more releases competing for the same spot. You must send your press release on a regular basis (every two months is usually enough) to the same editors. Editors sometimes decide to publish a press release they received six or seven times before, even if its copy remains unchanged.

A self serving press release that has little chance of being published (first page):

A.T.D. PHOTO WAREHOUSE

300 Main St. Anytown USA 12345 Tel (123) 123-4567 adt@email.com

For immediate release. No kill date.

Contact: Ann Louis

The Best Deals on the Internet!

If you happen to run out of film, or are in need of a new inexpensive camera, A.T.D. Photo warehouse is the place for you. "People are amazed at how low our prices are," says Robert Entrep, president of A.T.D. "The average photographer can save about $50 a year just by buying all his photo supplies from us."

A.T.D. Photo Warehouse (http://www........) carries everything a shutterbug needs: films (color, black & white, slides) of all major brands, disposable cameras, filters, lense cloths and much, much more. You can buy everything at wholesale prices — just purchase 5 or more rolls of films at a time.

Another thing you can find in the Web site is unparalleled customer service: A.T.D.'s knowledgeable staff is ready to answer all your photography questions through e-mail or chat programs. And if you are not connected to the Internet? No problem. A.T.D. will send you a brochure by land mail and take orders over the phone.

How do they do it? "Simple," says Entrep. "We don't have to pay exorbitant storefront rents, and we buy our merchandise in huge bulk. This is what a virtual store is all about!" But customers rarely ask how. "They come,

This release, for the same company, is much more professional and newsworthy (first page):

A.T.D. PHOTO WAREHOUSE

300 Main St. Anytown USA 12345 Tel (123) 123-4567 adt@email.com

For immediate release. No kill date.

Contact: Ann Louis

Amateur Photography: Any Questions?

"But my daughter doesn't have red eyes!" "But it was a new film — why are there spots all over this picture?!" "My office isn't green!" "Why do pictures shot in the morning come out bluish?"

You may have asked one of these questions yourself one time or another. You may have kept them to yourself. One thing is for sure — no amateur photographer is without his share of bad pictures. Unpleasant surprises reveal themselves on almost every roll of film developed. Photo lab employees are often too busy to give advice or answer your questions, and pharmacy salespeople (who simply send your film away to a third party to be developed) probably know less about the subject than you do.

Luckily, there are places on the Internet nowadays where you can get free advice and even a friendly team of experts to answer your questions. One of these sites is A.T.D. Photo Warehouse (http://www....), who, in addition to free advice, also offer a large selection of films, cameras and accessories at wholesale prices. "People come to our Web site to ask questions no one else would take the time to answer," says Robert Entrep, A.T.D.'s president. "It is amazing how one little problem can sometimes ruin an entire vacation. There was this person,

Please Reply

❏ We intend to use your press release on: _____

❏ We intend to use your press release sometime in the future.

❏ We will not be able to use your press release at this time.

❏ We will not be able to use your press release because:

_____

_____

_____

❏ We need more information:

_____

_____

_____

_____

Editor's name:

_____

Name of publication:

_____

A Reply Card

What Should Accompany the Release

You must include a *cover letter* with your press release. Cover letters introduce your company, Internet site, product, or yourself, and sometimes give the editor the gist of the press release. A good cover letter is short, succinct, and is written to get the *editor's* attention — not the periodical's reader, as the press release should.

A *reply card* can also be enclosed with the press release. This is an inexpensive way of knowing whether or not your press release was used. It may also be the only way, since most, if not all newspapers and magazines, never take the time to notify you of your press release's publication themselves. A reply card can be printed on the back of a postcard. There is no need to put a stamp on the postcard — editors seldom have to pay for their periodicals' mail expenses out of their own pockets.

Don't expect too many reply cards to arrive back at your mail box. The editors who will not use your press release will rarely send you a reply, those who *will* use it — maybe. But the few reply cards you will get are better than remaining in the dark and not knowing whether or not your press releases are any good.

Photographs

Enclose photographs if you have them. Your product, a related item, and even printouts of your Web site may add pizzazz to the text content of your press release. A photograph may also gain more space for your press release in the periodical. When enclosing a photo, make sure you follow these guidelines:

- **The photographs should be 4" x 6" or 5" x 7" glossy.**

- **The images must be clear.** Bear in mind that photographs lose much of their clarity once they are reproduced on the page of a magazine or newspaper (they will not be copied from a negative). Also, editors do not use bad photos, since these reflect poorly on their periodical.

- **Write your company name (as it appears on the press release's letterhead) on the back of the photograph** so that it will not get lost. Avoid using a ballpoint pen, which might leave deep marks that would be visible on the face of the photograph. Use a soft pencil instead.

Follow-Up

You can follow up on your press release with a phone call. Of course, to do this with every press release you send (and you should be sending about one thousand every couple of months) would be very time-consuming and expensive. Limit your phone calls to the most important contacts. Don't nag and never try to pressure the editor into using your release. This might backfire on you. Editors are busy people who value their time. It is best to simply inquire whether your press release was received (talk to the editor — not the operator).

Editors who try to tie the publication of your press release with your buying ad space in their periodical should be avoided. Serious periodicals with a solid readership seldom do this.

Media Mailing Lists

A good mailing list is central to a successful press release campaign (and also to a direct-mail campaign — see next chapter). You can either compile the mailing lists yourself or buy ready-made ones. To compile a mailing list yourself, the best thing to do is go to your local public business library. Look for the following directories:

▸ *Oxbridge Directory (a.k.a Standard Periodical Directory)*. This huge directory contains information for tens of thousands of magazines, newspapers and newsletters. Also available on CD-Rom (see page 112).

▸ *Directory of Publications* (Gale Research).

▸ *Newsletters in Print* (Gale Research).

▸ *Ulrich's International Periodical Directory*. (R.R. Bowker).

▸ *Literary Market Place* (R.R. Bowker). This huge directory contains numerous periodicals and other media. Although written to be used by the publishing industry, LMP will be helpful to you in finding the names and addresses of many newspapers and magazines in the U.S.

It is also a good idea to pick up a copy of the periodicals you are most interested in (e.g., trade magazines) and to write down the names and titles of the appropriate editor. You can also call associations and organizations relevant to your business or product and ask them for a copy of their newsletter or at least the name and address of the editor.

The number of publications from which you can compile a mailing list yourself is limited, and the search is very time-consuming (especially the part of retyping it all on your PC). A better alternative is buying the lists from a professional list compiler, or list owner. Mailing list companies usually send you the list on disk, with up-to-date data and sometimes even a guaranty. A guaranty means that you get a refund for every envelope above a certain percentage that is returned to you by the post office because of incorrect address/name. For example, if you bought 1,000 names and you have a 90% guaranty, this means that the 101st envelope that returns to you undelivered (and every envelope after that) entitles you to a certain refund (e.g., 25 cents per envelope). Another form of guaranty is the simple 60 or 90 days satisfaction guaranteed, where you may return the list within the specified guaranty period — no questions asked.

Mailing lists can be either bought or rented. When you rent a mailing list, you are allowed to use it only once, and instead of a floppy disk you receive peel-off labels. The list owner would know when the list is being used more than once because some of the addresses on the list are decoys — "planted" addresses belonging to the list owner himself that have been inserted for control purposes. It is usually preferable to buy a list since you will need to use it several times, and because working from a floppy disk will enable you to merge the list's database with documents you create on your PC (in other words, you will be able to personalize your letters).

Use the same list several times. Many prospects who do not reply the first time around respond to a second letter or even a third. Make at least three or four attempts before dropping a prospect's name from your list.

Mailing lists get old fast. Addresses change, people switch employers, new periodicals are added, circulations grow or decrease. It is a good idea to update your list once a year or at least every two years.

Possible sources for media lists are:

▶ **Oxbridge Communications, Inc.** 150 Fifth Ave., New York, NY 10011. Ph: (212) 741-0231, (800) 955-0231 Fax: (212) 633-2938, Web: http://www.mediafinder.com (you can download a demo version of their CD-ROM there). With over 80,000 periodicals, this is probably the largest database of U.S. and Canadian periodicals you can find. The price is rather steep for a beginning entrepreneur ($995 for the complete CD-ROM with all directories, or $695 for the printed version), but if you buy the CD you can construct lists in minutes according to criteria such as circulation, subject, staff position, printing specs, etc. This huge database can also be searched from their Web site, but the information displayed there is limited to names and telephone numbers only.

▶ **Bradley Communications Corp.** 135 East Plumstead Ave., PO Box 1206, Landsdowne, PA 19050-8206. Ph: (800) 784-4359, ext. 432, Fax: (610) 284-3704. They offer several lists on floppy disks, which can be ordered by subject (e.g., women's editors at dailies, consumer how-to publications). The complete directory, with nearly 20,000 editors at 5,800 media outlets (magazines, dailies, radio and TV, syndicates, wire services) costs $295. In addition to contact information, the listing for each media outlet also includes circulation, editor/position (usually several editors for each periodical), market size and more. Call for a brochure.

▸   **ParaLists.** PO Box 8206, Santa Barbara, CA 93118-8206. Ph: (805) 968-7277. Lists are sold by type of periodical (dailies, teens, religious, etc.). Ask for a price list. Keep in mind that ParaLists is geared to the publishing industry. You will not get editors' names here (except for book editors), nor circulation information. However, these lists cover a large number of magazines and newspapers, and are particularly helpful if you need only a few magazine subjects. Lists are rented for a one-time use on peel-off labels, or sold for unlimited use on disk.

It is important to use the editor's title when sending a mailed item to a periodical. For example, if you sell tax preparation software, your press release should be addressed to the Personal Finance Editor. If you have the editor's name, your press release will stand an even better chance of getting into the right hands. Avoid using a name without a title, however. If that person has left the periodical, your press release might be forwarded to him instead of reaching the editor that succeeded him.

Radio and TV

Just like the print media, radio and TV stations are looking for newsworthy stories. They can either invite you as a guest on a talk show, or run a story about your industry or product which will use your business as an example. If you have a conventional business and you do not offer a revolutionary new product or service, it might prove hard to get the broadcast media to take interest in you. Luckily for you, the Web is still news, and will probably continue to be so for many years to come. Presenting your business or product as a new Web feature (preferably with some free service for Internet users) will most certainly help you get media exposure. Remember that the features that the media find interesting may be what you consider secondary technical aspects of your site.

It is up to you to let the broadcast media know about your business. Send them a *media flier* — a short cover letter introducing a newsworthy subject on which you are an expert. As is the case with press releases, try to sell them a news item, not your business or your product. Your media flier should speak about popular trends, current news topics, upcoming events and such. Then, present yourself (or one of your employees) as either an expert or someone with a new/different angle on the topic.

Handling interviews requires practice. You have to anticipate hard questions and be ready with an answer. This means knowing your business inside out, of course, but it also means knowing the media. Read or listen to interviews with people in your line of business, and study the way the experts handle questions. For your answers to come out clearly and flawlessly, you have to rehearse them in the convenience of your own home. Use a tape recorder or a camcorder to check on your progress. You will have to work within the time frame of the show, whether it means getting to the point quickly or stretching your material over an hour. You should avoid using technical terms, mumbling, rambling, having a frozen expression, being negative, and above all, being too self-serving.

To be successful in getting radio/TV exposure, you must be realistic. Your chances of getting on *Oprah* are remote. You have to start at the bottom — shows at small radio stations. These can be either talk shows or special shows/spots dedicated to a certain subject (e.g., sports, investing, cooking). Once you collect a few interviews (and a few published press releases or press interviews), you are ready to approach larger TV and radio stations.

Starting with radio stations has one great advantage: many of the interviews carried out by them are phone interviews. You can give them from the convenience of your own home, without the need to travel and without the studio pressure.

Another thing you have to be realistic about is the effect an interview with a small station would have on the public. Don't expect your phone to ring off the hook or your server service to tell you they cannot handle the surge of traffic to your site. The main contribution of small station interviews is in helping you establish yourself as an expert and making it easy for you or your Web site to get a better exposure in the future. For this reason, you should think twice before traveling across the nation for an interview with a small, 20,000-viewer TV station. This is another reason why beginners should stick to radio stations and local TV stations.

Radio and TV stations are not supposed to charge you for interviews. Those who do have very small audiences, so you should not bother with them in the first place.

You can get broadcast stations' names and addresses from directories such as *Gebbie's All-In-One Directory*, *Bacon's* and *Working Press of the Nation*; all of these can be found in your public business library. You can also use Bradley Communications' broadcast media lists (see page 112).

Don't overlook newspaper and magazine interviews, which last longer than radio/TV interviews in people's minds (mainly because the magazines and newspapers themselves remain in their houses for several days). Some magazines have a circulation of several million readers.

Exhibits, Trade Shows and Conventions

This type of promotion works best when you have a new product to present to the public. It is especially useful when you are looking for a distributor for your product. Does a Web site count as a product? Sometimes. You would have to show exhibit attendees more than just new information or new images (on your site) in order to get their attention. Even if you succeed, the number of visitors to even the largest of exhibits is relatively small, and booths are usually expensive (and renting a booth is just the beginning — there are also hotel, travel, and booth design and construction expenses to consider). If you only expect the exhibit to help you attract new visitors to your site, renting a booth would not be cost-effective.

The good news is that you don't have to rent a whole booth in order to participate in an exhibit. There are two ways around it:

- **You can share a booth with one or two other exhibitors.** It is preferable, however, that your booth mates not be competitors. For example, a shoe manufacturer and a shoe polish manufacturer can share a booth, but two shoe manufacturers should not.

- **Often you will find associations or distributors that display items in their booth from small firms.** Contact associations or distributors in your industry to inquire if they can include your items or material at their booth. You can also call the exhibit organizers and ask if they know of exhibitors who offer such an arrangement. This option will save you a lot of money, time and headache.

Participating in an exhibit as an online-based business is a new concept. The main problem facing you is how to display your products, which are often online services or information, to the exhibit attendees. One way to go about it is by handing out brochures. This would be playing it safe, but it will arouse little interest in the average exhibit visitor. You need a gimmick to attract people's attention and make them want to take your brochures — you should not be selling the pastry, but the aroma. Even if your Web site is nothing more than a boring virtual hardware store, you still have plenty of room for innovative thinking. For example, your Web site can supply Internet users with instructions on making minor household repairs, or allow them to use a special software to try different color mixes (and see the results online on a virtual wall/piece of furniture).

Exhibit attendees must be able to view and use your site's features at your booth. A PC is a must, preferably with a very large screen, and it should either be connected to the Internet through a high-speed line, or contain all of the site's files on its hard disk. Allowing visitors to interact with your display is certain to attract many of them to your booth.

Instead of handing out brochures, which all too often wind up in the trash cans of the convention floor itself, try to take the visitors' contact information. That way, you can send them literature directly to their offices through land mail, e-mail and the fax machine. With this tactic, you are killing two birds with one stone: your brochures will not be disposed of right away, and the visitors' contact information remains with you so you can send them brochures and updated information whenever you like.

As mentioned above, you cannot expect an exhibit to expose your business to the masses. In online traffic terms, the direct result of even the most successful exhibit would be several thousand extra hits recorded by your site, and this by itself will not even pay for the costs involved in participating in such an exhibit. However — the most important thing to remember about exhibits is that they receive media coverage. If your display is innovative or interesting enough to get their attention, the sky is the limit. You can get news coverage, interviews, and lots of free publicity. In fact, a good (O.K., great) display can earn you more publicity than hundreds of news releases.

Where to find exhibits:

- *Trade Shows Worldwide* (Gale Research)
- *Trade Shows and Exhibits* (Rector Press Ltd.)
- Check with the trade or professional associations of businesses directly related to your product.

A few weeks before the exhibit or trade show is due to begin, make sure to send invitations (e.g., "See our booth at the .... expo") to key figures in your industry and to important business prospects.

> The business leads you develop in trade shows and exhibits cost you a lot of money — just figure out how much you spent on the exhibit and divide this sum by the number of leads. Never let them go to waste. Follow up on every such lead with literature and phone calls, and keep at it for at least several months.

Gifts and Point of Purchase Sales Aids

Unlike gifts to the consumer (see page 146), gifts to businesspeople are unsolicited in nature. In other words, the receiver does not choose to make a purchase or take part in a contest. Giving gifts to businesspeople is usually not an act of generosity, but an investment. Gifts to businesspeople fall under one of the following categories:

- **Gifts that are meant to be passed on to the consumer by the receiver.** For example, an online software vendor can contact several Web sites and (with their help) place a link in their site that allows visitors to download a free computer game. The Web sites displaying this freebie give their visitors something extra and so attract more traffic (especially if they add the keywords "free software" to their search engines' listings). The software vendor also attracts more visitors, who must visit his online software store in order to download the free software. You can also give other businesses (especially online vendors) promotional items to hand out to their customers. Let's assume that you sell baby accessories online. Bookmarks or mouse pads bearing your Web address and a short description of your online shop would be good promotional gifts that baby furniture stores (especially online) can give their customers.

- **Gifts for the businesspeople themselves.** A good example of such a gift is a calendar or a desk organizer with your business name printed on it. Gifts of this type should be given to businesspeople you are working with on a regular basis and also to prospects and people you hope will recommend your Web site or products to their business associates. Not only will such a gift help them remember you, but the gifts themselves might prove to be effectual promotional tools. Imagine a calendar with your business name and URL hanging on the wall of an accountant's office. Dozens of people would see this ad (for this is what it really is) every day. If your site sells books about investing, chances are at least some of this accountant's customers will take an interest in it.

Point of purchase sales aids are not normally used to promote online or mail-order businesses. However, if you sell your products through conventional retail channels as well as online, you might want to send counter displays or banners to stores that carry your product.

Notice Boards

"Find your traveling companion online. Http://www......" This notice was posted on the notice boards (also called bulletin boards) of at least a hundred camping gear stores. It was printed on a small quarter-page note, and the cost to the advertiser was nothing more than a few gallons of gas. Yet this unassuming ad brought in thousands of dollars' worth of sales to the advertiser, who was running an online travel agency combined with a bookstore (dedicated to travel guides). This entrepreneur had incorporated a public service — a free online service for finding travel companions — into her site, and used it to attract potential customers.

There are dozens of notice boards strewn over every town in the world. You can find them in small pharmacies, colleges, schools, specialty stores, doctors' offices, barber shops — the list is endless. All you need are a few small notes and a car. Ask the proprietors for permission to post your notices. It is usually not a problem if:

- You are not promoting a competing business.

- You are providing a needed service for the patrons, preferably for free.

- Your note does not have a sales pitch — this is a public service.

Word of Mouth

In many industries, word of mouth is responsible for more sales than advertising and media coverage combined. People tend to believe their friends, coworkers, and relatives more than they do media stories and reviews, and a lot more than they believe commercial advertisements. Visitors to your Web site may not always make a purchase, but if your site is interesting enough, your product or prices impressive enough, they will remember you. Sooner or later, a friend, coworker, family member or an acquaintance will bring up the subject of your site (e.g., sports equipment) in a casual conversation. The visitor who was impressed with your site is bound to say something about it, and even recommend your site to his interlocutor.

Word of mouth promotion should be taken seriously, which means that you have to invest in it in the following ways:

- **Your site should contain as much information as you think your customers might want to see, plus a little more.** Text, pictures, software, links, audio and video clips — if your visitors can use it, give it to them. You want your visitors to be repeat visitors and to refer more potential customers to you. If you are sending prospects information packages through the mail, make sure you do not skimp on material. Successful direct-mail merchants send people who respond to their ads whole booklets and sometimes even audio cassettes.

- **You should offer a responsive and helpful customer service,** which should assist not only potential customers, but also people who ask general questions about your industry or product. The best tool for such a customer service is e-mail, which allows you to answer questions at your leisure (unlike the telephone or chat programs).

- **Should any of your customers experience problems with your products or services, don't leave them hanging.** Deal with the problem quickly and efficiently even if this means refunding the customer's money. Be courteous at all times.

- **Give people incentives to spread the word.** For example, one online bulletin board used to offer a 50% discount to anyone who brought in a customer. Other incentives you can give people who bring in new customers are gifts and special privileges, such as access to a members-only section of your Web site.

Not just individuals or businesses, but even the media can find you through word of mouth. For example, a journalist who is looking for people to interview for a story about online real-estate agents might ask his colleagues to help him find such individuals. One of these colleagues might turn out to be an editor who received your press release three months earlier, and who did not find it appropriate for publication in her newspaper. The same press release that failed its primary mission can thus lead to an interview with another editor at a different paper. The more contact you have with the media, the more likely your name is to be mentioned in their circles. Some entrepreneurs send monthly letters to their trade and industry publications announcing that they are available for interviews, and enclosing clips from previous interviews and published press releases. Editors often ignore such notices (which sometimes accompany press releases) until the need arises to use them. Chances are that in a period of one year, at least one editor at one periodical will decide on interviewing the entrepreneur who has sent these notices.

Vocal conversation accounts for most word of mouth promotion, but there is also e-mail (which can quickly replace the telephone as a means of communication between businesses) and newsgroups. Remember, however, that unsolicited direct e-mail advertising is <u>not</u> promotion by word of mouth, even if it pretends otherwise (e.g., "Here's a great site I visited yesterday"). Forget this principal, and you risk generating negative, instead of positive, word of mouth.

> The cliché, "Say what you will about me so long as you spell my name correctly" may hold true for film or book reviews, but not for word of mouth promotion.

Magazine Articles

Writing magazine articles about your industry or market implies that you are an expert, and gives you credibility and prestige. It is undoubtedly one of the best ways to promote yourself and your business. The trick, of course, is getting your articles published.

For starters, forget about the high-circulation periodicals. Until you establish yourself as an expert, you should court only small magazines and newsletters. You can find the addresses of many of them, as well as larger magazines, in *Writer's Market* (F&W publications). Each entry includes contact names, a short description of the publication, and often its policy and guidelines for writers. For other lists of magazines and newsletters, see pages 110, 112.

You must convince magazine editors not only that your articles are well-written, useful to their readers, and to-the-point, but also that *you* are qualified to write them. In the editor's view, the fact that you sell motorcycle parts and accessories online may not be enough to qualify you as a writer of an article about motorcycle maintenance. What you should do (were you to have this problem) is:

- **Post a few articles you have written to your site,** together with other free information and tips on motorcycle maintenance. This will help convince the editor that your site is an information center and not simply an online store.

- **Write a short résumé stressing your experience as a motorcycle mechanic.** As with a real résumé, it would be helpful to make a mountain out of a molehill: every experience you have ever had in your life that is even remotely connected to motorcycles must be magnified (but not lauded). This is also the place to mention any writing experience you may have.

- **Enclose supporting documents with the articles you submit:** diplomas; letters from satisfied clients (for consultation services, not sales); published press releases; academic essays you have written; interviews. Some people also include a photograph of themselves with prominent figures in their field. You will be surprised how often this subliminal tactic works. Even if you do not have such pictures, a photograph of yourself would add more credibility to your submitted work.

- **The best means of persuasion is previously published articles.** Once you have these, your chances of seeing your articles published will increase dramatically. Creating such a track record is hard at first, but with a little perseverence you will find that fewer and fewer of your articles are being rejected.

Don't count on the income from magazine writing to send your kids through college. Small periodicals seldom pay for articles. When they do, the amounts are somewhere between $10 and $50. As a promoter, this should not matter to you one bit. Your goal is getting bylines, not collecting compensation.

A *byline* is the author's name that appears with the article. It can also describe the author's qualifications for writing this article. For example: "The writer is chief motorcycle mechanic at XYZ Motorcycle World, http://www......" When querying a magazine, mention that you want a byline, and waive any payment.

Once you have written an article, you own it. The rights to the article are yours (even if you did not file it with the Library of Congress) until 50 years after your death. It is a piece of property you can sell or even leave to someone in your will. Anyone wishing to publish your article must get your prior permission. If a magazine is interested in publishing your article, they will send you a letter specifying their terms and ask your permission to use it, or in other words obtain the rights to your article. The most common types of rights are:

- **One-time** rights. The periodical has the right to use your work one time, and with no exclusivity. You can sell or give the rights to the same work to other publications.

- **First serial rights.** Same as the above, but with the understanding that the periodical buying the rights will be the first to publish it.

- **All rights.** The periodical buying all rights becomes the new owner of the work. You are not allowed to sell it to anyone or even to use it yourself without permission.

- **Exclusive rights.** You are not allowed to sell or give the rights to your article to anyone else for a predetermined period. You still own the work, however, and the magazine cannot sell the rights to it.

According to a 1978 law, anyone paying you for using your written work without specifying terms is assumed to have bought one-time rights for it. You will find that periodicals do not like to buy one-time rights from new writers. Many of them will ask you for at least an exclusive. As they often will not publish your articles otherwise, it is a good idea to agree — at least until you are an established writer. However, try not to sell all rights since you will lose your article.

When querying magazines, try to avoid multiple submissions. Editors don't like it when the same article you've sent to them has also been mailed to 20 other magazines. Send a cover letter with your article informing the editor that this is the only magazine this article is being submitted to, and that you will wait four weeks for their decision before you send it to the next periodical.

If your article is still being rejected after you've queried several magazines one-by-one, you may want to save time and send it simultaneously to several magazines. Make sure, however, that you mention the fact that this is a simultaneous submission in your cover letter.

Submitted articles must be double-spaced and have a 1.5" margin on all sides. When querying high-circulation magazines with busy editors, try to send only a description of the work instead of the whole article. If the editor is interested in the subject, she will ask to see the entire work. Always enclose a reply card and a return envelope (or a postcard) with your query.

> About 99% of articles submitted to magazines by beginning writers are rejected. You must learn to come to terms with these odds and be persistent and patient.

Catalogs

If you have a product that is not available in stores, such as a homemade product (e.g., of a decorative value), you might want to consider placing it in a mail-order/phone-order catalog. These catalogs are arranged by subjects (gardening, cookbook software, candles, etc.). You can find a list of more than 14,000 such catalogs in *The Catalog of Catalogs* (Woodbine House). Catalog houses will not allow you to display your Web address in their catalog, but you can usually attach a small brochure with this information to the product itself. For example, if you sell fish-tank equipment, you can use the small tag that is attached to the product to invite the buyer to visit your site. This will give you the opportunity to show (and possibly sell) buyers more products and give them information on fish-tank maintenance which will help turn them into repeat visitors.

Sponsoring Local Events

From children's sporting competitions to spelling bees, local events can mean good publicity to the sponsoring business. Since yours is an online business, you should also set up a special site dedicated to the sponsored event, which will be accessible from your business site's main directory (but any mention of your business must end here — this special site is not the place for you to plug your products or services). For example, you could open a home page for your neighborhood high-school basketball team, which will display the players' photographs and personal information, as well as statistics and other relevant data. The players' relatives and friends are bound to take an occasional peek at this page, and this is a great way of attracting hundreds of local visitors to your site. This would be a particularly good idea if you sell items that appeal to high-school students.

Trademark Gifts

Some mail-order retailers and manufacturers routinely enclose special symbolic gifts with each product they ship out to customers, and also with subsequent mail-order offers. One auto-diagnostics center used to send customers and new prospects a small plastic lemon as part of their "Don't get stuck with a lemon" sales pitch. This is a great way to stand out from the crowd and etch your business name in the memory of your prospects. The gift must be related to your product or service, and must remain unchanged for at least several years.

Making Your Competitors' Advertising Budget Work for You

Here is a simple way to take customers away from your competitors: accept their coupons, and make it known that customers will get from you the same discounts or incentives others offer in their ads. This promise, which you can announce in your Web site, direct mail and magazine ads, will go a long way towards winning you new customers. Although it sounds magnanimous, this tactic will actually save you money: your competitors' advertising budget, which is invested in promoting their special deals and discounts, will now work for you, too, and bring *you* more customers. Some retailers even cut their prices to cost in order to attract new customers. After all, new customers are often repeat customers, and you can also add them to your mailing list.

Other People's Clients

Occasionally businesses find themselves unable to handle all the work they get. Often this is because of seasonal work pressure (as is the case with CPAs) and sometimes the cause is a shortage of personnel or tremendous market growth. If your business is in the service industry (retailers do not have an overflow problem since they can always order more products), you may want to call your colleagues and competitors and inform them that you are available to handle all the customers they must turn away anyway. A referral fee will probably tip the scale in your favor and convince the business you contact to cooperate with you. Remember — a business that refers customers to you would have had to turn them away anyway since it already has all the work it can handle. For these businesses you are a savior, not a moocher — thanks to you they get a small fee instead of nothing, and do not have to turn down customers. The benefits for you are obvious: in addition to the immediate business you get, you start building a customer base for your company.

Maintaining Contact with Your Customers

Most businesses invest substantial amounts of money in trying to turn prospects into customers. Yet, amazing as it may sound, many of these same businesses never spend a single penny on people once they do become customers. A customer base is your most important asset; don't forget them and don't let them forget you. Send them a letter three or four months after they have made a purchase or used your services, and thank them for their business. It might also be helpful to enclose a little gift. For example, you might send a small booklet with recipes or a pen with your business name on it. Holiday greeting cards are especially good public-relations tools. Some entrepreneurs have even sent their customers birthday-greeting cards (this required that they obtain their customer's date of birth through a special questionnaire first). Not only will such gestures turn many of your customers into repeat customers, they will insure that their friends and family hear about you, too.

Another way of building a loyal customer base is by rewarding repeat customers with frequent-customer points (or credits). Every purchase is worth a certain number of points that can be accumulated towards a free gift (typically one of your products) or a discount.

Questionnaires

Questionnaires do a lot more than just remind customers of your existence. They give you much needed feedback, and let you know what it is that you are doing right (or wrong). Questionnaires should address three main issues:

- **Your product or service** (quality, price).

- **Your customer service,** including order taking and handling, answering customers' questions, delivery speed.

- **Your advertising:** where did they first hear of you? Did they find your ads informative?

A good questionnaire must also ask: "Will you recommend us to your friends?" This question should only come after a series of questions concerning the quality of your product/service. As a matter of fact, all of your customer-satisfaction questions should lead to this one question. Having given your product and service a high rating, the customer will find it hard not to answer "yes" to it. You might think that this answer by itself does not guarantee that the customer will actually tell his friends and family about you, but research has shown that giving a promise in writing has a subliminal effect on many people, and may increase the chances that your clients follow through on their promise. At any rate, having a customer spend time writing (and thinking) about your business is certainly worth the postage expenses involved in this project (a pre-stamped envelope *must* be enclosed with a questionnaire). Many businesses (Citibank, for one) have even gone as far as to enclose a dollar bill with their questionnaires to show they appreciate the customer taking the time to answer them.

No good questionnaire is complete without a few lines dedicated to customers' suggestions. Many business owners will tell you that some of the best marketing or business suggestions they have heard and implemented came from their customers.

> It is important to send questionnaires not only to customers but also to non-responders. Prospects who have **not** replied to your *sales letter* (see pages 143-151) can teach you a lot about the way you are marketing and selling your products. Use the feedback you get from them to improve your sales material or advertising copy. Since they are *not* your customers, it is doubly important to give such prospects an incentive to fill in your questionnaire.

Unconventional Ways to Deliver Your Message

Sometimes it is all in the delivery. Prospects, business contacts, and anyone else whose attention you want to get expect to be contacted through either the phone, the fax machine, e-mail or land mail. Use the element of surprise. Contact them in unconventional ways to receive their undivided attention, if only for just a minute. Remember: Western Union still sends telegrams (call 800-325-6000, then press 2, 3), couriers still hand-deliver letters, and an envelope delivered by U.P.S. or Federal Express will receive more attention than one delivered by the U.S. mail. Some people even prefer to drop by in person to deliver sales material to important business contacts.

A great way to stand out from the crowd is by recording your message on an audio or even a video cassette, and sending it instead of a letter. Video presentations are an especially good sales tool since few people will chuck the cassettes in the garbage without watching at least a few minutes of what is on them.

A manufacturer of computer accessories had tried in vain to interest one of the big home-electronics chains in his products. That company's CEO never read the printed material this entrepreneur had sent him, and even ignored a video cassette with a presentation of the product. To get this prospective client's attention, the entrepreneur had resorted to what may seem to be an anachronistic tactic: he sent him the presentation on super 8 film, and enclosed a super 8 film projector. Needless to say, that prospect watched the film the minute he received it, and called the entrepreneur that same day to arrange a meeting.

E-mail Signatures

Signatures are short text files that you can have automatically attached to your outgoing e-mail messages. In addition to your name and contact information, the signature may contain a slogan, business description, or any other data you choose to include. Entrepreneurs have even used signature files to introduce new products or services. Anyone you send e-mail to — clients, suppliers, prospects, business associates — will be able to see this data even though the e-mail message itself does not contain sales material. This is a good way of using e-mail for promoting your business without "spamming."

Let Others Talk about Your Business

Word of mouth takes time to develop, but you can get people to talk about your business and to send you new customers right from the start. Some of these promoters will gladly do it for free — your family and friends. With others, things are not going to be so simple, but it is still possible. Many entrepreneurs hire people (especially students) to spread the word about their business. This is done both online (through e-mail, chat rooms, discussion groups) and off (through conferences, associations, clubs, on campus, etc.).

You have to distinguish between word of mouth and professional referrals. For example, let us suppose that you paint portraits from photographs. You can, of course, contact photographers and offer them a referral fee for every customer they send you (which is a good idea by itself), but to generate word of mouth promotion, you need disinterested parties (satisfied customers, acquaintances, art students, etc.), not associated businesses that act as your representatives.

Another way of making people talk about your product or service is by giving it to them free of charge. Of course, you would not last long were you to offer these giveaways to just anyone. You should only hand out your products to influential people: editors of college newsletters, key figures in your industry, distributors, local radio DJ's and so on. So it doesn't look as if you were trying to bribe them, you should enclose a letter with your free sample that would say something along the lines of: "... As you are an expert in this field, we value your opinion and welcome any input you may have.... In appreciation of your help, please keep the enclosed product. If you like it, please tell your friends about it."

Show You Care

In today's social climate, it never hurts to be politically correct or involved. Donate a certain percentage of your sales to worthy causes and don't neglect to announce it on your Web site and through your ads and brochures. Consumers like to buy from a business with a social conscience. You will also make your customers' decision to buy from you a lot easier if you let them know that your products are made from recycled paper, that you recycle film rolls, that your products would not harm the environment, and so on.

If you are trying to reach the local market, working with local charity organizations can be a great source of positive publicity for your business. Furthermore, this may even help you build a customer base in the long run. For example, if you give free legal consultation to low-income senior citizens, it is probable that many of them will refer their wealthier friends and relatives to you.

Business Cards

Business cards may very well be your most cost-effective method of promotion. They are very cheap to print, and you can leave them with practically everyone you meet. While it is true that the vast majority of these cards quickly find their way to the waste basket, the few that manage to survive will more than pay for your effort. It is also a good idea to enclose business cards with sales material, literature, and letters to business contacts and leads. People rarely keep sales letters, queries or brochures that they do not take immediate interest in, but business cards often fare better thanks to their small size and ease of storage.

> Once in a while, even the most untidy of businesspeople will sort through the various business cards that have accumulated over the years, and throw away the least interesting ones. To make sure your card survives this selection, make it unusual: choose a smart color scheme; try unorthodox material (e.g., plastic instead of paper); have important, useful data printed on its back; use optical illusions, and so on.

Would Anyone Care to See a Picture of Your Corporate Headquarters? You Bet!

Well, the truth is, it's not that anyone really wants to know what your office building looks like. Few will give a picture of this building a second look. However, the subliminal effect is what's important here. Many businesses include a small picture or photograph of their office building/plant with their letterhead or sales material. While the readers hardly notice such a picture, they nonetheless tend to take the business that sent the letter more seriously. The same approach works equally well online: with a picture of an office building on your home-page, your business would seem more established to online visitors.

Networking

Networking allows you to bounce ideas off of other business people and colleagues, learn of new developments in your industry, get inspiration from other entrepreneurs, develop business leads, and much more. One way to network is by joining trade or marketing associations in your industry. You can also do a lot of networking by attending trade shows and exhibits (even if you do not rent a booth or display your products there), and by joining local chambers of commerce.

Public Relations Companies

If you prefer to leave most of the promotion to someone else and to concentrate on other aspects of your business, another option is to turn to a public relations company. Some of them offer only consultation services; others will also do all the legwork (and office work) for you. Prepare to shell out large sums of money should you decide to take this course.

> Even if you do decide to hire a PR company, never assume that because you are paying someone else to take care of it, promotion is "No longer my job." You should always be on the lookout for new opportunities for promotion and publicity.

7

ADVERTISING AND MAIL ORDER

Tell people that you are running a mail-order business and the first thing that will come to their mind will be: "Must be a great feeling to find checks in your mailbox every day." Well, it is. However, you must not forget that you will also be sending checks to the mail boxes of other businesses — particularly ad agencies and various periodicals. Also, there is the tense, long wait to see whether or not your ad has produced any results. Mail-order is a great business, but not necessarily an easy one.

The following three questions will determine your future in the mail-order business:

1. "Do I have the right product?"

2. "Can I write ads that sell?"

3. "Can I find the right periodicals to place these ads in?"

Question 1 was already discussed in length in Chapter 4. Now we come to questions 2 and 3 — the most important aspect of a mail-order business: the ad.

Classified Ads

Writing effective ads is an art rather than an exact science. Inevitably it is also a process of trial and error. When pressed, some of the most successful ad agencies (who charge an arm and a leg for their copywriters' services) will tell you that only one-half of their ads achieve the desired result. You would expect such experts to score a little better than 50%, but as it turns out, manipulating the public's cravings and desires is no child's play.

A good ad is an ad that sells, period. It does not have to make people laugh, or cry, or say "wow!" It does not have to get people thinking, and it does not have to make them happy. These are all means to an end. A large telecommunication company tried once to run very funny TV commercials that were supposed to sell their products and services. In a subsequent survey, this company learned that, while people considered these commercials very funny, they did not always associate them with the advertiser's name.

A copywriter should be a salesperson, not a novelist. Some of the best ads ever published consisted of no more than a picture and a few words (but then, a picture is worth a thousand words). When sitting down to write an ad, ask yourself the following questions:

- **Why would anyone need my product?**

- **Assuming that people do not need it, how can I convince them to buy it anyway?** After all, if people only bought what they truly needed, only real-estate, food and pharmaceutical companies would remain in business.

- **Is there a dream I can sell?** For example, when you sell beer, you are not selling a golden, bubbly liquid, and you are not even selling taste. You are selling a sense of relief (from trouble, heat, loneliness, suffocating routine), hope, and self-esteem. You are selling a mood.

- **Can I describe my product or service as "new," "innovative," "revolutionary,"** or any other term which implies that the product is not the same old item consumers can easily get at their neighborhood store?

There are two basic types of ads: *classified ads* and *display (or space) ads*. Classified ads are cheaper, and do not involve graphic design or artwork. Classified ads are the best way to test out your material. If they prove successful, it's time to move up to the much costlier display ads. If not, the classified ads can be changed and this experiment would only have set you back a couple hundred dollars. Many successful mail-order companies started with classified ads, and many of them still use them today, along with display ads.

Here are some rules for writing effective classified ads:

- **Think about the one thing that will make potential customers buy your product:** price, new technology, making his or her life easier, etc. Now describe this one thing in a single short sentence. A catchy opener will get the prospect's attention, and once this happens, half the battle is won. For example: "Like pets? Raise dogs for a living." or "Miniature surveillance video cameras $149.95."

- **Make sure the headline appears in bold letters.**

- **High-ticket items do not sell well through classified ads unless the ad offers *free information*.** For example, an ad that reads:

  Model hot-air balloon — stays airborne for hours! Send $12.99 to ...

  will not pull well since people are wary of sending too much money to companies they do not know. It's better to write:

  Model hot-air balloon — stays airborne for hours!
  For free information ...

Consumers are much more likely to purchase a high-ticket item (yes, even $12.99 is high for classified ads) from a catalog or a brochure you will send them. This, of course, gives you the opportunity to describe your product over several pages, and to add pictures. Although you only paid for a classified ad of two or three lines, the free information approach allows you to expose your potential customers to several pages of your best sales material. If you want to sell high-ticket items directly from a magazine, use display ads. Items sold directly through classified ads should be in the range of $1 to $4. Most successful mail-order firms use the free information approach, which also allows them to expose potential customers to a selection of products rather than just one.

- **Try not to use a post office box in your address.** Unless you or your company are household names, this makes people suspicious. A Web address will make you appear more established and serious, and so will an 800 number

- **Remember, in a classified ad, you are paying by the word.** Each word must be carefully considered. Don't write what you think is necessary, but what you think you can't do without. For example, the ad:

    Learn how to grow expensive plants for high profits. For free information, send to A.B.C.D.E. Enterprises, [address]

can easily be shortened to:

    Grow expensive plants. High profits. Free information.
    A.B.C.D.E.   [address]

The ad lost nothing from its clarity or effectiveness, and your gain is eight words that you won't have to pay for. If you were to run this ad in *Popular Science*, for instance, this would translate to a savings of $110.80 per issue, or $1,329.60 a year! Even your address should be shortened as much as possible. If you decide to use a post-office box number for your address, it is better to rent a box at the post office itself rather than from an independent mail service. That way, you can omit the street address and give only the box number. Simply write: "box", the city, state and zip code. For example: Box 34567, Anytown, Anystate 12345 (and don't forget your Web address).

• **Talk directly to your prospective buyer.** For example, if the previous ad had read:

> How to grow expensive plants. High profit. Free information. [address]

this would have communicated a sense of aloofness toward potential customers. This is an archaic, lifeless style that is rarely used by ad copywriters today. The ad should read:

> Grow expensive plants. High profits. Free information. [address]

• **Make the prospect want to know more about your product or service.** Your ad should imply that the free information you send contains very interesting and useful data.

• **Your ad should not be preachy or condescending.** Avoid lines such as: "I will teach you how to lead a better life."

• **The ad copy must be clear, simple and sincere.** Avoid big words, riddles or patronizing, self-absorbed wisecracks (e.g., "If you like being poor, don't reply to this ad.").

• **Make your ads look believable.** Ad copy that reads: "Be a millionaire by the end of this month!" smacks of fraud.

- **Give the prospective buyer the feeling that he cannot get the product or service you sell anywhere else.**

- **Practice.** Write several versions of your ad copy, and show them to (objective) friends and acquaintances, and maybe even to a few strangers. Always compare your copy to that of successful ads (see ahead).

- **Check your competition's advertising.** Can you offer something they don't?

- **Pretend you are a potential customer reading your ad.** Does the ad insult your intelligence? Does it make you curious enough to request information? If the ad does not convince you, it will probably fail to sway others.

- **And finally, the most important piece of advice for mail-order entrepreneurs:** once you have decided on a magazine you want to run ads in, buy both a recent copy and an old one (five to six years old). You can get old copies at your public business library, or by contacting the magazine itself. Find the listing under which you want your ad to appear (e.g., Business Opportunities, Cable Equipment, Apparel) and compare the classifieds from both issues. You are bound to find at least a few ads that have remained virtually unchanged throughout this five-to-six year period. Those are the successful ads — ads that perform so well the copywriter never dared to change them. You may want to clip out and save a few of these ads. Don't copy them verbatim, but try to emulate their style, approach, and choice of words. You can also learn from ads that appear under other listings — different products often use the same sales pitch.

These are some of the magazines commonly selected by mail-order companies to run ads in:

Popular Science
Popular Mechanics
Income Opportunities
House Beautiful
Popular Photography
Popular Electronics
Outdoor Life

Of course, there are hundreds of magazines and newspapers you can advertise in. Normally you should choose the magazines your customers are likely to read, and a few high-circulation, general-interest periodicals. It is a good idea to experiment with a few publications until you find the ones that produce the best results.

Magazine salespeople will tell you that one ad is not a good gauge for measuring a publication's effectiveness, and that you should place it at least three or four times to even come close to the ad's full potential. While this is often true, that approach would make comparing several magazines a very costly affair. You are better off running one ad one time in several magazines and comparing results. Don't expect the first ad to even cover its cost, but discontinue running it in magazines from which you only receive a handful of replies.

When placing an ad in a magazine, expect to get only 20% to 50% of replies during the first month. The rest of these replies will stretch out over several more months, and you should not be surprised to receive replies as late as one year after publication. An ad is considered a good ad when it brings in 2½ times its cost. This means that even a good ad cannot be expected to bring in more than its cost during its first month. First ads usually do poorly, but (once you find the best publications for them) you should persevere and continue to run them. The same ad will pull better after several months, and may not reach its full potential for up to a year. Once you have found your niche, the right product/service, and the best periodicals to advertise in, persistence is central to success.

When running test ads in several magazines, you will no doubt lose two or three months while evaluating the magazines' pulling power. This is a necessary evil, but it also allows you to change your ad copy should the results from *all* magazines prove too disappointing (and remember — if a first ad brings in 25% of its cost during the first month, this is not so bad).

How would you know which magazine is responsible for an order or a reply to your ad? The simplest way to determine this is by adding a department number to your address. For instance, you can write your P.O. Box number as "Box 1234C." In this example, "1234" is your real box number, and "C" is the magazine code. By assigning different codes to different magazines, you can determine whether an order or a request for more information came from *Popular Mechanics* or *House Beautiful*. Keep your codes short (one letter is best) or prospects might realize that they are not part of your box number or address and omit them.

Mail-order businesses are seasonal. You will find that replies to your ads dwindle during the summer months (when everyone is on vacation) and peak from September into November (before the holidays). The winter is considered a good period for mail-order businesses as people tend to spend more time at home and read (or at least browse through) magazines and newspapers.

Most mail-order companies run their ads all year round. However, if your budget is small, you can allow yourself to skip the worst pulling months. As a rule, it is always a good idea to place your *first* ad in one of the best pulling months (remember — a first ad is not only *your* first ad, but also any ad that sells a new product or one to which you have made changes).

Dailies do not pull well. The main reason for this is that their life span is very short — people read the newspaper, then throw it away. Magazines, on the other hand, are kept for much longer periods, often in a special rack or tucked away on the shelf. Also, since magazines are published only once a month, their readers tend to take their time reading them. The result is that a magazine often lies on a kitchen counter or living room table for a week or two, neither out of sight nor out of mind.

Your Information Package

When you run ads that promise free information to potential customers, planning this info package is as important as planning the ad copy itself. Once a prospect sends you a reply to your ad and requests that information, you've got one foot in the door. Your mission now is to open this door further. Your tool is your information package, which is really a sales letter. Keep the following tips in mind for writing effective sales letters and putting together useful information packages:

- **The fact that you are not limited to a few lines (as is the case with an ad) does not mean that your sales letter has to be long and verbose.** Imagine opening an envelope you have just received through the mail and finding a sales letter that contains many lines of text with few gaps and no graphics or images. Such a letter would probably put you off and you wouldn't read it. A sales letter must be eye-pleasing and inviting to read, with short paragraphs, bold subheads strewn over it, and a few images. A nice color scheme can also help.

- **Avoid overusing the exclamation mark (!).**

- **Never send prospects a brochure that describes your product or service without enclosing a personal letter with it.** In a personal sales letter, you will be talking to the potential customer and not at him.

- **Remember that prospects who send you inquiries through the mail probably do not have access to the Internet,** or they would have used the URL printed in your ad and visited your site. The sales material you send these people must take this fact into account. For example, never refer them to your site for further information. Also, avoid using computer or Internet terms or jargon.

- **A sales letter should not be too formal or commercial.** It must radiate a friendly, comfortable atmosphere so that the reader is relaxed, lets his guard down, and becomes more susceptible to your ideas.

- **Make sure your sales letter is free of spelling errors, and that the copies you mail out are clean.** Use only a high-quality copy machine, a laser printer, or an offset printer for printing them.

- **Once you believe you have come up with an acceptable copy, put it aside and get back to it only a couple of days later.** You will be surprised at how many mistakes (in style, sales approach, etc.) you will find and how many new ideas you will have. Novelists, painters and other artists constantly use this method to view their work more objectively. There are painters who put away their finished work and completely ignore it for as long as a year before they look at it again. By the time they do, they become open-minded, almost uninvolved viewers.

- Once you have captured the prospect's attention and convinced him that your product or service is right for him, the next thing your sales letter must do is **ask this person to act.** Even though this seems redundant, you must ask the prospect to make the purchase. An incentive will not hurt either (e.g., "Send the enclosed order form by April 5th, and pay only $29 instead of the regular $39").

- **Say your last word *after* the end of the letter by adding a P.S.** Use this P.S. to mention something important, such as a guaranty, a second bonus gift (see ahead), or another important piece of information about your product.

- **Testimonials increase sales significantly.** Use excerpts from letters sent by satisfied costumers in your sales letters and brochures. Don't sit back and wait for these letters to accumulate on their own — solicit them. Send questionnaires to your first customers asking them what they think of your product. Write again to those who were satisfied with it and ask them to describe what they liked about the product. Ask also for their permission to use their answers and names in your sales materials. Most of the people who liked your product will be happy to do so.

- **Avoid writing everything there is to write about your product in your sales letter.** Leave some material for a brochure or a circular that will support the sales letter.

- **A self-addressed return envelope must be enclosed with the package.** Placing stamps on return envelopes (either by hand or with a postage meter) is very expensive and usually unnecessary. You should either let the prospect pay for the postage (which most mail-order companies do), or use a postage-free business reply envelope. When using this kind of envelope, the post office will charge you only for the envelopes that are actually sent back to you. The postage for a business reply envelope is more expensive than for a regular letter, but as you would be paying for a smaller amount (than if you placed a stamp on all the envelopes you enclosed with the information packages), this is certainly worth it. Contact your local post office for more details.

- **A money-back guaranty is a must.** It lets the prospect know that you believe in your product, and increases the number of orders you will get. A long-period guaranty (six months, a year) is better than the usual 30 days since it does not put unsatisfied customers under pressure to return your product immediately. Many unsatisfied customers will thus put off returning your product until they forget about it. When you refund a customer's money, you only need to return what he paid for the product — the customer is responsible for any delivery charges.

- **It is common practice for mail-order companies to offer a bonus gift with every purchase.** The bonus gift is usually related to the product being sold. It should be mentioned on a separate, colorful note that is enclosed with the package. A separate note is more effective and noticeable than a mention of the gift in your sales letter, and it also allows you to change the gift without having to rewrite your entire info package.

> Some mail-order companies add the line: "If you don't like our product, return it for a full refund but keep the bonus gift," or: "We want to give you a free gift just for giving our product a try. If you don't like our product, return it and keep the gift!" These generous offers usually result in a higher reply rate to direct mail offers, and only a few prospects take unfair advantage of them.

- **Send inquiry letters to successful mail-order companies that offer free information** (see page 140). Study their sales material carefully. Pay attention not only to the content of this material, but also to the style in which it is written, the layout, color scheme, use of catchy phrases, overall tone, etc. The way the information package is arranged is also important: how much information is given in the sales letter? The brochure? The circular? Study even sales material of mail-order companies outside your industry. Mail-order companies who have been around for years must be doing something right.

Some mail-order companies send prospects literature on more than one product. Although this can increase sales, make sure that all the products you sell are related, and that the product for which the prospect has requested information tops the bill. You will not score many points with the recipient if the brochure or sales letter she asked for is hidden among a dozen other brochures that flaunt different, irrelevant products.

A Reply Card

To order, please fill in this form and send it to us in the enclosed envelope.

Yes! Send me your booklet. I understand that this guide will ship via Priority Mail (in the U.S. only). I also understand that there is a six-months money-back guaranty for it.

Price: $19.95 + $3.00 for shipping (New York residents add $1.65 for sales tax).

Name: _____

Street address: _____

City: _____

State: _____

Zip code: _____

Country (if other than U.S.A.): _____

Enclosed is my ❑ check ❑ money order for $_____ payable to [name] (no cash, please).

Charge to my ❑ Visa   ❑ MasterCard   ❑ Amex   ❑ Discover

Credit card no. _____

Expiration date (mm/dd/yy): _____

Signature _____

TYCLE Resources

Dear Friend:

Wouldn't you like to have an extra $1,000 in your pocket at the end of the year? Wouldn't you like to get this $1,000 <u>every year</u>? You don't need to get a second job or cut down on your entertainment budget. All you need do is make simple, easy repairs to your own car!

Let's say that your alternator breaks down. A rebuilt alternator costs about $40, and yet, if you go to a mechanic you will most probably be charged $100 or more for this repair. Installing an alternator is something you can do in fifteen minutes or less. In other words, you can make $60 in fifteen minutes! Another example: a tune-up for most cars costs between $140-$200, yet the parts needed can be purchased for as low as $50.

During the course of any one year, even a reliable car requires several visits to a repair shop for oil changes, tune-ups, minor repairs and general maintenance. All these add up. If you happen to own a used car, and especially if you have more than one vehicle in your household, you are probably paying over a thousand dollars a year for the above repairs.

All you need for making such repairs yourself are about $100 worth of tools, a few weekend hours, and my manual.

My manual will show you how to save money <u>right away</u>. No more visits to your mechanic except for major, complicated repairs (and I'll show you how to tell whether or not your car needs such a repair). No more having to accept what your mechanic tells you (and having to pay for it)! No more second-rate parts installed in your car without your knowledge when you are paying for original ones.

Have no time to study the manual? No Problem. My manual is composed of separate, independent sections, each dedicated to just one car problem. You only need to refer to the relevant section when you have a problem. An easy-to-use troubleshooting table at the end of the manual will help you locate the source of the trouble in no time (see the enclosed circular for an example). It will even teach you to understand "car language" and to know which rattle or noise signifies an impending malfunction.

Easy-to-understand step-by-step instructions, diagrams and illustrations show you how (with the help of your car service manual) you can fix almost anything for only a few bucks.

You will feel great, as I and many other automobile owners do now that we take care of our own car maintenance. You will learn how to spot serious problems long before they occur and prevent them. You will have more money to spend on appliances, clothes, entertainment, vacation or anything else you cannot afford now. You will also be able to fix all these small, annoying defects that make your car harder to sell.

So, use the enclosed order form and reply envelope to order your copy of the **Be Your Own Mechanic manual** now. Don't be caught without it the next time your car breaks down!

P.S. If you are not <u>fully satisfied</u> with this manual, you have <u>six months</u> to return it to us for a full refund — no questions asked!!

[signature]

A bonus gift certificate

Bonus Gift!

Order the *Be Your Own Mechanic* manual, and receive the *Inexpensive Parts Dealers Guide* free of charge. This state-by-state 38-page directory shows you where to get the best deals on new, used and rebuilt parts for your car. Save hundreds of dollars, and even sell parts yourself for extra income.

Make sure you respond quickly to inquiries. Prospects who have to wait two to three weeks for your information package to arrive will assume that the product itself will take even longer. Furthermore, three weeks is a long enough time for the average person to lose interest in your idea.

Designing the envelopes you send to prospects is an art of selling unto itself. Unusual wrappings command attention and are usually spared the fate of the plain white envelopes that wind up in the waste basket without as much as being opened. Unusual envelopes add pizzazz to your sales material and can make even avid junk-mail haters take a peek inside them. There is no wrong way to design an envelope so long as the post office agrees to deliver it (make sure you check with them first) and the prospects find it interesting. Use your imagination to come up with a unique idea. For example, you might try envelopes resembling aluminum foil, envelopes of unusual shapes (round, triangular, etc.), or envelopes with provocative messages printed on them.

> A New-York-based entrepreneur has sent half-envelopes to his potential customers. He cut regular 10" envelopes in half and sent only one side (glue-sealed at the "open" end) to prospects. As a result, he saw a 20%-30% increase in the reply rate.

Dealing with prospects who reply to your ads online is a totally different ball game. Here, you don't have to send prospects sales material through the mail. This has its pros and cons. On the one hand, you save money on postage and printing expenses. On the other, you have little contact with these prospects, who visit your site without leaving their names and addresses (unless they buy your product). This means that you cannot compile a mailing list of prospects as you would with snail-mail replies. The material prospects find online should be different than that which you send by land mail. The Internet community seeks content, not hyperbole. Also, the Internet allows you to add colorful images, links and other goodies to your sales material.

A mistake commonly made by mail-order/Internet entrepreneurs is giving the URL of their site's home page in their ads. The home page contains a directory and general information, both of which are directed at visitors of all kinds. The information package for prospects only appears as one item in the home page's directory. The prospect is often confused by this, and finds it hard to correlate the ad with the site. The URL that appears in your ads should therefore be that of a separate, special Web page that is dedicated only to the subject of the ad. Use your imagination to make this page even more inviting and interesting than the sales material you send through the mail. Don't forget to set up a counter for this page (contact your server service for this purpose), which will tell you how many prospects respond to your ad (bear in mind, however, that this information can never be accurate, since a prospect who has visited the page twice will be counted as two visitors).

Display Ads

Display ads are not for the beginner. Wait until your classified ads prove themselves before you move on to display ads. The rule here is simple: if your classified ads work, a good display ad will increase your sales; if your classified ads are a flop, a display ad, being more expensive to run, will increase your losses.

It is important to add a photograph or an illustration to your display ad. Any picture you send to a magazine must be clear and of high quality — even a good picture loses some of its clarity when reproduced on a magazine page. An illustration is often clearer than a photo, especially in small ads.

You can plan the layout of your ad yourself. Buy copies of mail-order magazines and study their display ads. Start with small 1/12th page ads, which many successful mail-order companies use. Design the ad around a picture or illustration. The picture should usually appear at the top of the ad, but you might want to deviate from this rule if you think the overall layout looks better with the image at the bottom or center. You can also use an ad agency to design your ads. Make sure they have experience in mail-order display ads, which are slightly different from regular display ads (for stores or products that are available at retail outlets). Magazines and other periodicals might also help you design your ads, but you will get a lower rate if you send them camera-ready artwork.

Display ads allow you to sell high-ticket items directly from the ad — prospects do not have to request information from you first. However, these potential clients might still want to know more about your product or service before they place an order. Your display ad should include a telephone number (preferably a toll-free one) in addition to your address and URL. A few prospects will contact you through e-mail, but as the vast majority of the population does not yet have access to the Internet, expect to handle most inquiries on the telephone. You can hire an answering service with live operators to handle the calls if you are unavailable to take them yourself. The answering service will take the caller's number and allow you to return the call in your own free time.

> Moving on to display ads does not mean that you have to abandon your well-pulling classified ads. Many successful mail-order companies run both kinds simultaneously.

Since ad agencies receive a 15% commission from magazines and periodicals they place ads in, many advertisers have created their own in-house ad agencies. These advertisers (who pay only 85% of the ads' cost) save thousands of dollars a year with this tactic. The problem is, many periodicals will not give the 15% discount to in-house agencies. These periodicals will check the ad agency's information against that of the advertiser. If the companies' name, telephone and fax numbers, or even e-mail address are the same, the periodical will assume that this is an in-house agency and charge it the full rate.

If you are acting as your own in-house agency, or if you deal directly with a periodical, you must send them an *insertion order*. An insertion order is a letter that you enclose with the ad copy and artwork, and which includes the following information:

- Insertion order number
- Advertiser's name
- Date of insertion
- Ad size
- Section of the magazine where the ad is to appear
- Number of times (or months) the ad is to appear
- Rate (less discounts for frequency, ad agency, or cash payment)
- Special instructions
- A description of the product (if required by the periodical)
- Any other information required by the periodical

Per Inquiry Ads

Per inquiry ads do not cost you money up front. As their name suggests, you only pay the periodical per inquiry, or order, which means that the periodical processes the orders for you (you cannot display your own address in the ad) and charges you a certain percentage of the sales (usually 30% to 50%). You send the product to the customer, and receive a check from the periodical. Per inquiry ads are run by small periodicals who need to fill unused space. This deal is also offered by a few small television and radio stations.

Periodicals and other media offering per inquiry deals will not accept just anyone. You have to convince them that your product will sell well and that your ads will pull.

Are per-inquiry ads worth it? On the one hand, they save you money. You need to pay the periodical/station only for the items you have sold. On the other hand, since all of the magazines and stations that offer per inquiry deals are small, your ads will not reach a large audience. Furthermore, if you are successful with per inquiry ads, you will be better off with regular ads, which do not take a large cut of your gross sales.

Direct Mail

Many mail-order companies do not run any ads in magazines, but use direct mail instead. As the name suggests, direct mail campaigns bring your ads directly to the homes of prospects. The sales material you send to a prospect's home is almost the same as the info package you send prospects who reply to your magazine ads. All the elements are here: the sales letter; the circular or brochure; the self-addressed envelope; the bonus gift certificate; the reply form/card. There is only one difference: when you reply to a query letter from a prospect who has seen your ad in a magazine, this prospect already has a vague idea as to the content of your information package. For instance, people who send for more information on the *Be Your Own Mechanic* manual already know that you offer to teach them how to save money on car repairs and maintenance, and they're interested in this material. When you send *unsolicited* information packages to prospects (direct-mail), you don't know whether or not they are interested in the type of product you sell.

Or do you? Enter mailing lists. Mailing lists are pre-sorted by demographic data or areas of interest. For instance, if you want to sell the *Be Your Own Mechanic* manual, you will need a mailing list of people who own used cars (which are more likely to require frequent visits to the repair shop).

You can find mailing-list owners and brokers in *Direct Marketing List Source, Klein's Directory*, or in local Business to Business directories (see page 111 for more information on mailing lists). You can also buy/rent lists from magazines and other periodicals.

Unlike the mailing lists for media contacts discussed in Chapter 6, mailing lists for individual prospects often comprise tens of thousands of names or more. Naturally, these lists are more expensive, and should therefore be tested before you sink a lot of money into them.

To test a mailing list, you should first rent a small part of it from the dealer (see page 111 about the difference between renting a mailing list and buying one). Start with 500-1,000 names. Since he knows you are testing his list, the broker might try to rent you only "the crème de la crème" of his mailing list. To minimize this risk, ask to rent only the names beginning with a certain letter, or only those which reside in a certain (small) state.

> Mailing lists are expensive to buy, but even more expensive to use. Sales material printing expenses, postage and even working time can easily cost $5,000 for a list of 10,000 names. Never trust a mailing list until you test a small part of it and make sure it works.

Before you even test a mailing list, try to find out how old it is. As the average American family moves once every four years, even a two-year-old list might be too old. The broker must give you a guaranty that at least 90% of the names and addresses on the list are up-to-date (in other words, the list should be 90% deliverable).

Selling through direct mail has two clear advantages over selling through magazine ads:

- **Your prospects are not exposed to competing offers.** In magazines, your ad appears right next to your competitors'. Prospects who receive your sales material through the mail will find it harder to compare your products or prices with those of your competitors.

- **Your competitors cannot see your ad when you are using direct mail.** They do not know what your prices are, and it makes it harder for them to copy your product or selling method.

You are not allowed to sell the mailing lists you buy to third parties. However, once a prospect orders something from you and becomes your customer, this customer's name and address belong to you. Over time, you will be able to compile your own mailing list of such customers. Since *this* list belongs to you, you can sell it — you now have another product to add to your selection. You can sell mailing lists directly to businesses like yours, or use a broker to sell them for you. You will need several thousand names on your list for a broker to take an interest in it. To compile good lists, make sure each entry includes the following information:

- ▸ Customer's name
- ▸ Customer's address (including zip code)
- ▸ Date of purchase (at least last purchase)
- ▸ Any additional information you can gather, such as age, sex, occupation, number of people in household, and payment method (credit card or check)

The post office has a special bulk rate for mailing large quantities of envelopes, which can save you thousands of dollars a year. One of their requirements is that you bring them the mail pre-sorted by zip codes. Contact your local post office for more details.

Card Decks

A card deck (or pack) is a collection of a few dozen business reply cards which are sent (in one envelope) to prospects in the same way as individual direct-mail letters. Participating in this kind of mailing gives you the following advantages over sending your own individual sales letters:

- **Your cost is slashed significantly,** since many other advertisers share the mailing expenses.

- **You leave the printing, envelope stuffing, mailing, and list maintenance worries to the card deck company,** which gives you more time to concentrate on other methods of promotion.

Of course, there are also a few drawbacks:

- **You cannot test a sample of the mailing list the card deck company uses** prior to using it.

- **Your card competes for the prospect's limited attention** with a few dozen other cards (even though they do not sell the same item).

- **The small, postcard size reply card you will have to use means serious space limitations.** A card deck does not allow you to pitch your product in the same way that you would with a sales letter or brochure.

   To find card-deck companies, consult the *Business Publication Rates and Data Directory* (Standard and Data Service) at your public business library.

Radio and Television

Effective radio and TV commercials are usually priced out of the reach of most small entrepreneurs. To tackle this field successfully, you need either a lot of experience in this type of advertising, or the help of a hired expert. Due to the large amounts involved, any miscalculation or oversight here might spell doom for your business.

   You can, however, experiment with small, inexpensive stations. A few community-access television channels allow businesses to become sponsors. Although they will not air your commercials, your business name will be mentioned several times for a certain fee. Is this a good advertising opportunity for your business, or a complete waste of money? Only common sense, knowing your market, and maybe even a small test will help you find the answer to this question.

Cold-Calling and Telemarketing

You can use your telephone to generate sales in two ways:

A. By calling individuals (cold-calling, telemarketing).
B. By calling businesses (follow-up).

Giving your sales pitch to individuals over the phone is very hard work. It requires you to start with a good calling list (similar to a mailing list), and to prepare a convincing, yet short (20 to 30 seconds) opening speech to follow the mandatory "How are you today?" line. To achieve perfection, you will have to practice for hours and try your sales pitch on friends. You should sound natural, and not as though you are reading your lines off a page. You also need perseverance and patience. You will hear far more "No, thank you," than "Yes."

It is not likely that you will have any time left to run your business should you choose to do the calling yourself. Telemarketing companies will be happy to this for you (usually for an up-front fee plus a percentage of the sales or a per-call charge) and will provide the marketing representatives. Telemarketing companies offer two basic services: *inbound telemarketing*, where marketing representatives take calls from prospects who reply to ads and commercials, and *outbound telemarketing*, which means that the representatives initiate the calls to the prospects (cold-calling).

> Before you invest a fortune in professional outbound telemarketing, make a few hundred sales calls yourself to determine whether or not telemarketing is right for your product.

The second target group you can reach by phone is businesses (volume buyers, wholesalers, etc.). Here you should only initiate a call as a follow-up on a lead — no cold-calling. For example, if you have sent letters to local distributors all over the United States trying to convince them to carry your product, you should follow up on these letters with a telephone call. You must be polite, succinct, and most important of all, you must find the golden path between persistence and aggressiveness — no one likes to be bothered. The best approach is to call prospects during the time when they are most relaxed; never call just before, or just after lunch, and avoid calling people on Mondays. When prospects answer the phone, simply ask them whether they have received your letter. If the answer is yes, ask them what they think about it. Three possible scenarios may ensue:

- **The prospect requests more information,** which you send and then follow up on again with a second phone call

- **The prospect accepts your offer or starts negotiating with you.**

- **The prospect rejects your offer flat.** Learn how to handle these rejections politely — you may contact this person or business later. Keep on sending sales letters (with improved terms or prices) to a business that has rejected you and follow up with a telephone call. Even the same product at the same price might be accepted by a contact that rejected you only a year before: the market may have changed, that business's needs might have changed, or, as will often happen, after a whole year in which you maintained contact with them, your prospect begins to take you more seriously.

Leads to follow up on can be generated through sales letters, exhibitions, conventions, referrals or advertising.

> Never call a business contact at his or her private home unless invited to do so.

Faxes

Unsolicited advertising through the fax is illegal in the United States. Violators can be reported to the F.C.C., who will fine such businesses or individuals. Even if this practice were legal, using fax paper someone else has paid for to print your ads on would not win your business too many friends.

You *can* use the fax machine for promoting your business, however, by including your Web site address on your letterhead. Although this does not sound like much, it can produce very good results when sending faxes (e.g., cover letters, query letters) to the media, or when answering a customer's question through the fax. You can also send faxes to subscribers who have agreed that information be sent to them in this way. This is not much different than maintaining an online mailing list (see page 30). For example, you can fax a monthly update on your industry (or related subjects) to your subscribers, with your own business information added to the bottom of the page.

Advertising on the Web

Web advertising is still at its infancy. The advertising industry is yet to come up with a fool-proof method for checking the effectiveness of online ads. The "classic" online ad is a very small "hot-key" banner ad — a one-slogan ad that visitors are supposed to click on to be transferred to the advertiser's site. The advertisers can then give such visitors more details (plus a sales pitch) on their products or services. The main flaw with this strategy is that it fails to take into account the weariness of Internet users. New users, still curious about all aspects of the online world, will occasionally click on such hot-key ads; old users, who have seen every Web gimmick imaginable, will only click on ads that really interest them.

The other approach to online advertising is making online ads larger, and more similar to magazine ads. Such ads, whether they include animation, video clips or plain text, are more noticeable than the above banner ads. Since they have less space limitations, they can convey more information about the advertised product or service. Of course, the user can click on special hot-key areas of these ads as well, but their main goal is to be seen or read — not necessarily to bring potential customers to the advertiser's Web site. This approach, which is more conventional than the previous one, has one drawback: it is harder to find sites that will display these ads because they take a lot of space and are unpopular with Internet users.

Another tactic, still in its experimental stages, is called *push* or *channeling* (and sometimes *push-channeling*). It means displaying ads for Internet users whenever they log onto the Internet. In other words, the user does not have to visit a certain site to be exposed to this type of advertising — ads appear as long as he is online. Of course, the user must first download a special software to enable his computer to receive these ads. Why would Internet users want to download such an application in the first place? The key is the "you" approach: the same push channel that displays commercial ads also brings users useful information such as news updates, financial information, game results, and various other goodies. You can join existing channels (try to find those that offer users information related to your product or service) or start your own. If you start your own channel, you will have to provide users who download your push application with your own information/news service on a regular basis, which can be a daunting task. For names and URLs of companies that provide push-channel services, use the words "push channel" (or "push+channel") with one of the search engines.

With the recent proliferation of commercial Web sites, the supply of online advertising space now far surpasses the demand. While high-traffic sites charge hundreds, and sometimes thousands of dollars per week for a small banner ad, many smaller sites charge only $10 to $20 for the same ad. Some do not charge any money and opt instead to place a reciprocal ad at the advertiser's site. To make sure a site has enough traffic to justify the cost of placing an ad there (even for $10), contact independent Internet evaluation and measurement companies (see page 65 for their names and Web addresses).

The best places on the Internet to place your ads are related sites and zines (online magazines). You can find a list of the latter at Ecola Newsstand (http://www.ecola.com/). They have links to hundreds of zines and conventional periodicals with an Internet presence.

Handing Out Fliers

Although the effectiveness of this method for promoting Internet-based businesses is yet to be proven, many online vendors have been known to do this. Of course, your seeds should be sown on fertile ground. If you sell laptop computers or business software, the World Trade Center or another business district would be the right place for handing out your fliers. There would be little point in distributing these fliers in the fish market.

As with any other form of advertising, fliers should have a hook. They must get the readers' attention in two to three seconds or they'll wind up discarded. Freebies or special sales combined with catchy or provocative headlines should do the trick. Try them on your friends and family members first, then print an initial test quantity of two or three thousand. If you get a good response, move on to larger quantities. If not, change your flier. If even this fails to produce results, can the whole idea and move on to other promotional methods.

Flier distributers are usually paid minimum wages, and are relatively easy to find. However you will have to check on them periodically to make sure your fliers are not deposited in bulk into the trash can by your employees. Also, make sure they offer the fliers to passers-by (somewhat aggressively) rather than just stand on the street corner waiting for people to ask for one.

Teaser Ads

The art of teasing can be effectively applied to the advertising world. To illustrate this point, here's a conventional, non-teaser ad:

> Make your own soft drinks at home! Just pour water and concentrated juice into our UltraSoftamatic 2000, and you'll have a bottle of great tasting soda in seconds! Drink all the soft drinks you want for just pennies a bottle!

This ad copy might pull very well as it is. However, since newspaper readers are exposed to hundreds of ads in any given week, this ad might slip their minds a few seconds after they read it. Now let's suppose that the advertiser chose instead to place a rather large display ad with just one sentence hanging in the middle of it, reading:

> **A soft drink manufacturing plant in your own home for $19.99?**

This question remains unanswered. At least in this issue of the newspaper. The next issue shows the same ad, or one with slight variations. Now readers take notice of the ad, and become very curious, if even a little mad at the advertiser for keeping them in suspense. Two issues later, the same ad appears with the addendum:

> **See next issue for details.**

By the time the next issue of the magazine or newspaper comes off the press, you can be sure that a large number of readers will be browsing through it looking for the promised details. This "end-of-series" ad will be treated almost as a news item, and will pull much better than had it not trailed the teaser ads.

To help readers recognize the next ads in the "series," you'll want to add a small logo or image (nothing too revealing) to all the ads. It will also help if they all appear at the same place in the periodical (e.g., near a certain column).

You can use the same tactic with a direct-mail campaign. Simply send prospects one or two teaser letters before the real sales letter arrives in their mail box. For example, you can send postcards with one mysterious sentence printed on the back. With direct mail it is even more important that the same logo appears on all the mail items in the series. It is likely that the final letter in the series will not be treated as just another unwanted piece of junk mail.

Yellow Pages

One of the most basic forms of advertising is also one of the best. Of course, some businesses will benefit more than others from this advertising medium. If your business offers subscription to online services, there is little point in using the Yellow Pages to tout for it. For most businesses, however, an ad there can boost sales and bring more customers to their Web site. Although it is still not commonplace, the number of advertisers who display their Web addresses in their Yellow Pages ads is growing every year.

The main problem with this form of advertising is that your ad copy cannot be changed for a whole year. For this reason, it is best to use the Yellow Pages and other business directories only to advertise general information about your business or product. Special sales and offers, and anything of a temporary nature do not belong there.

Placing Ads on Packages

Let's assume that you sell flea collars for dogs. Where will you advertise your product? Since only about 35% of U.S. households own dogs, an ad in a general interest newspaper or magazine would be wasted on 65% of their readers. This means you only get 35% of your advertising money's worth. Advertising in magazines that cater to dog lovers would be much more cost-effective, since nearly 100% of their readers own dogs, but most dog owners do not read these magazines.

Now consider placing ads on packages and wrappers of dog items and food. The public exposed to this type of advertising is made entirely of dog owners, *and* almost all dog owners buy these products.

Advertising on packages of related items is therefore an efficient way to reach your potential customers. You can place your ads either on the package itself, or inside the box (e.g., on a circular or card that is attached to the manufacturer's instructions). When negotiating with manufacturers or retailers, you can offer them either money or reciprocal ads (on the packages of products you sell). Some manufacturers or retailers will even agree to place your ads on their products in exchange for a special service or a free gift you will give their customers. Since you have an online-based business, you can also provide such customers with free information they can find in your site.

The same piggyback tactic applies equally well to the service industry. You can use related businesses (but not competitors) to deliver your message to their customers. A New York film developer has sent sales material for other, related businesses such as T-shirt printers, custom-calendar makers and photo-retouching artists to his customers (together with his own material). Directing all inquiries and replies to himself, he then charged these companies a referral fee.

Summary

The 5 Most Important Things to Remember about Running a Business on the Internet

- Running a business on the Internet is not akin to playing a computer game, where all that is required of you is to hit the right keys on the keyboard. You will have to use offline, conventional methods as well to promote and run your business. Ask yourself, "How am I going to promote my business?" and not, "How am I going to promote my business *online?*"

- Good Internet/mail-order entrepreneurs spend 50% of their time promoting their business and the other 50% thinking about how to better promote it. Promotion is the name of the game.

- Think of an Internet-based business as a real-world business first, an online business second. You should go with any idea that will make you money, whether or not it has anything to do with the Internet.

- It is not the number of hits your site records that counts, but the amount of money it makes (directly or indirectly).

- If you take orders only on the Internet, you cut off 90% of your potential customers.

AFTERWORD

An Internet-based business is first and foremost a business, and as such must be promoted in every effective way, *both online and off.* Realizing this is crucial to success in (online) business, and I sincerely hope that this book has brought you one step closer to this success.

If you are running a business on the Internet, you have probably already gathered some valuable experience that may help other Internet entrepreneurs succeed. If you have a piece of advice to share with the rest of us (if it is valuable, it might be included in future editions of this book), or if you have any comments on this book, please e-mail them to home@actium1.com (include the word TIPS in your subject line), or send them to the following address:

Actium Publishing.
1375 Coney Island Ave., PMB 122
Brooklyn, NY 11230

Ron E. Gielgun

Raising the Dough

Assuming your bank account is not overflowing with excess funds, and that the bank-of-dad has closed its gates, you will need to find other sources for working capital. You have several options:

1. Banks. These are the institutions whose business it is to loan money to entrepreneurs. However, banks like to play it safe and may prove a very hard nut to crack. They require tax returns for two or three years, references, a good credit history, or, if the applicant fails to show all these, good collateral. Of course, some banks are more friendly towards small businesses and new entrepreneurs than others, so it is worth shopping around for a while.

The Internet is a new, unproven grounds for banks, who consider online businesses very risky (plus there is very little banks can take from them should they default on the loan). It has been said that restaurants, filmmakers, and publishers have the hardest time of all getting a bank loan. As an Internet entrepreneur, you will find that your job is even harder. If your enterprise is a combination of conventional and online businesses (as recommended throughout this book), try to downplay the online part and concentrate on the more conventional aspects of the business.

If you cannot get a business loan, try instead a personal loan from your bank. The loan amount will probably be smaller, and you — not your business entity — will be responsible for paying it back. However, for these exact reasons getting a personal loan is a little easier than getting a business loan.

2. Other lenders. These sources of capital include private lenders, credit unions, and life insurance companies. These lenders tend to be more flexible than banks, but most of them charge a higher interest rate (unless you take a home equity loan).

3. Pawn shops. Although this option seems to be taken right out of a Charles Dickens' novel, pawn shops still exist and can be used to turn a family heirloom, old furniture, jewelry or other pieces of bric-a-brac that are gathering dust in your basement into available cash. Of course, if you have an object that you would not be too sorry to part with, simply sell it. You will usually get more than a pawn shop would give you for it.

4. If you find it hard to borrow money from your friends and family, consider selling them shares in your company instead. That way, the loan — a word that causes nervousness in many people — turns into a business investment. The advantage of choosing this option is that you will not have to worry about returning a loan. The obvious drawback is that you must share your profits with somebody else.

5. If you cannot find a friend or a family member to invest in your new business, you can always seek venture capital. Many financial institutions, businesses and even individual investors are constantly on the lookout for new investment opportunities and are willing to take a greater risk than most lenders. Of course, you will have to convince them that your business plan is solid, that you are the right person for the job (unless you hire a business manager), and, most important of all — that you are going to make them rich. Venture capitalists expect a very high return on their investment.

Finding an investor for your company requires a lot of leg work and perseverance. You'll also want to hire a professional to prepare a business plan for you, which can be very expensive. In other words, if you fail to get a loan for your business, do not expect finding an investor to be a stroll in the park.

6. The Small Business Administration sometimes guarantees up to 80% of business loan amounts for qualifying small businesses, which is usually enough to convince most commercial lenders to approve your loan application. To check if you qualify, contact them at (800) 827-5722 or through their Web site (http://www.sba.gov).

7. Credit cards. Last but not least, credit cards can be a great source of unsecured loans for the beginning entrepreneur. If your credit limit is $10,000 to $20,000 or more, you already have a considerable pre-approved loan for your fledgling business. The main problem with credit card loans is their exorbitant interest rates, which may sometimes be as high as 21% or more. Luckily, many credit card issuing banks occasionally offer promotional rates which can be as low as 6.99%! If you have at least two or three major credit cards, chances are you have already received some of these promotional offers by the mail. If you never did, apply for cards that do offer such deals (usually the larger issuers). While some of these promotional rates last for only a year or so, there are credit-card issuers who will give you the low rate for the life of the loan (any payment to the credit-card company will apply first to the low rate loans and only then to the rest of your balance, so that the loan is paid off first).

Appendix B

Methods of Marketing

If you sell products (either through mail-order or on the Internet), chances are you are planning to be a retailer — someone who buys goods from a distributor or manufacturer and sells them to the end user. There are, however, other ways to market your product, which are worth keeping in mind:

1. Selling to Distributors/Wholesalers. If you have a product that you manufacture yourself (this includes homemade artifacts), you can try to sell this product through wholesalers and distributors. Of course, you don't have to give up your direct sales approach — wholesale revenues can supplement your existing retail income.

Finding a distributor is not easy and may take many months of correspondence, phone calls, meetings and tireless promotion. A good distributor will ask for exclusivity, and may require you to keep large stocks of the product and provide customer service. They will, of course, take a substantial piece of the pie, which will include their share and the stores' profit, but they sell in large quantities. If you dream of turning your mom-and-pop operation into a million dollar enterprise, this is the path you should take.

2. MLM (Network Marketing). MLM, or Multi Level Marketing, is a relatively new (30 years old) method by which products are sold through a hierarchical chain of distribution.

Compare the two distribution-chains diagrams on the next page. While the conventional structure relies on a single, predetermined chain of distribution, the MLM structure allows for endless possibilities. At each level, there are people who are at the same time salespersons and distributors. Each node in the structure can sell directly to consumers, but they can also find other, lower levels to sponsor, from which they receive a commission for every item sold.

1. A conventional chain of distribution

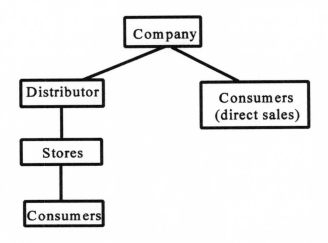

2. MLM

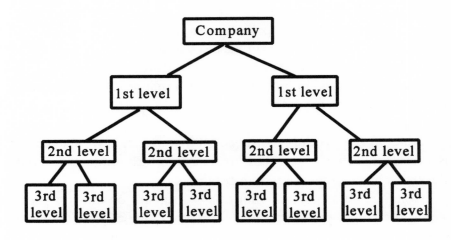

For example, let's say that a person in level one sells products (which he buys from the company) to the public. Now this person recruits another person, for whom he is the sponsor. This new person is in level two. The sponsor, in level one, earns a certain commission (5% to 10%) on the products level two sells. When level two recruits another person (level three) both he and level one earn a commission on level three's sales, and so on. Of course, every salesperson/sponsor can recruit as many people as they wish. In theory, as the number of levels (and people in each level) grows, the company (at the top level) can make a fortune without having to promote its product.

Sounds like a pyramid scheme? Well, it sometimes is. In the United States, MLM is legal only as long as it has a legitimate product and it does not involve unethical practices. For example, taking a high registration fee from every new recruit is unethical, because such an MLM company would be deriving its income not from the sale of its products (which would benefit the salespeople as well) but from the salespeople themselves. Another practice that smacks of fraud is promising new recruits that they will make tens of thousands of dollars in a matter of a few weeks.

MLM takes years to produce substantial income for the individual salesperson, especially on lower levels. Most MLM companies claim that MLM does not involve selling, but the truth is, selling is *central* to MLM success. Good salespeople who persevere and know how to recruit other hard workers can make a living in MLM, but it would be months or even years before they could quit their day jobs. As many MLM companies admit themselves, about 99% of new recruits fall short of the goal they had set for themselves, and leave the MLM business for good.

The advent of the Internet has blown a new wind in the MLM's sails. Both MLM companies and salespeople/sponsors on every level believe they can now recruit new down-line salespeople with minimum effort. Their favorite tools are unsolicited direct e-mail messages, and unsolicited posting to newsgroups, both of which are regarded as spam. But as salespeople on every level in every MLM company (and there are thousands of these) tried to recruit as many "down-liners" as they could, the Internet became awash with billions of junk e-mail messages, millions of unwanted newsgroup postings that have all but driven away the newsgroups' traditional subscribers, and tens of thousands of MLM Web sites that use every gimmick in the book, legitimate and otherwise, to attract visitors. The outcome of all this is that recruiting new salespeople is today harder than ever. If you are thinking of dabbling in MLM or even make it a serious business, make sure you have income from other sources to support you during the first hard years. Your chances of making a quick buck from MLM nowadays are remote.

MLM's greatest advantage is the fact that the company has to spend very little on advertising to sell its product — this job is done by the down-line salespeople. However, successful MLM companies have a long-term view, and what they save on advertising they invest in perseverance and patient waiting.

3. Drop-Shipping. If you are short on cash and prefer to invest the working capital you have on promotion rather than inventory, you can drop-ship your way to retail success. The drop-ship arrangement works like this: you sell a product through advertising, direct mail, or online, and take the payment. You then pay the factory or wholesaler that stocks the product, and *they* ship it out to the customer. In many cases, the drop-shipper will even take the payment for you, leaving you to concentrate on the actual selling. It is a win-win situation where you don't have to keep an inventory and the drop-shipper gets more business without having to invest further in advertising. Make sure, however, that the drop-shipper leaves you a large enough cut to survive and grow (by further investment in advertising). The important thing to remember is that you are not the drop-shipper's salesperson — you are an independent company with its own overhead and advertising expenses to consider, and you should be paid accordingly.

The Internet allows you to become a drop-shipper at minimum expense. If you have a product or a service you want to sell, you can contact other companies or individuals with Web sites and reach a drop-ship agreement with them. They will place your products' pictures and description on their site, and sell them for you. They can also link this sales material directly to your site and have you take care of the payment as well as the shipment. Amazon.com, the largest online bookstore, has been doing this successfully for years (you can reach them at http://www.amazon.com).

4. Consignment. When you sell your products through stores, and they pay you only for the items that have been sold, you have a consignment agreement. This method's two greatest disadvantages are:

- You have to tie up large inventories before you realize any sales.

- Retailers will tend to push the items for which they have to pay in 30 to 60 days rather than those for which they only have to pay once they are sold.

Why, then, would anyone want to sell his products through consignment? For one simple reason — to get a foot at the door. Stores don't like to do business with one-item manufacturers and often lack shelf space for any new product. Without offering consignment, your chances of selling to them (and reaching their customers) are remote.

If you are an online/mail-order retailer, and small manufacturers contact you and try to sell you their products, always try to take them on consignment. This will allow you to expand and add to your inventory while saving your purchasing budget for items that have already proved themselves.

Useful Links

Traffic measuring services and online advertising agencies:

Doubleclick http://www.doubleclick.net

I/PRO http://quantum.ipro.com

PC-Meter http://www.npd.com

Promotion:

Oregon State University
http://www.orst.edu/aw/stygui/propag.htm

Link Master http://linkmaster.com

American Demographics Inc.
http://www.marketingtools.com

Leading Learning Fountains (awards)
http://www.tricky.com/lfm/awards.htm

Who's Marketing Online http://www.wmo.com

Virtual Promote http://www.virtualpromote.com/home.html

MediaFinder from Oxbridge Communications (lists of

newspapers and magazines) http://www.mediafinder.com/

Entrepreneurs' resources:

Internet Business Start-Ups
http://www.actium1.com/

Babson College (Gopher) http://gopher.babson.edu

Entrepreneurs on the Web
http://www.eotw.com//EOTW.html

How to Start a Business
http://www.inreach.com/sbdc/book/index.html

Entrepreneur Weekly http://www.eweekly.com/news

Inc. Online. The Web magazine for growing companies.
http://www.inc.com

Services for online businesses:

La Sierra University http://www.lasierra.edu/~willgurn/dlist

PositionAgent (monitors web site search engine rankings on
top search engines) http://www.positionagent.com

Reaching Gopherspace, Veronica and Archie:

Global Commerce Link
www.mac.net/net2/internet/internetrsc.html

Checking the availability of domain names:

InterNic http://rs.internic.net/cgi-bin/whois

Issuers of online currency:

DigiCash http://www.digicash.com

Cyber Cash http://www.cybercash.com

What's New services:

WebCrawler http://webcrawler.com/select/nunu.new.html
Choose "Add URL" to include your site.

Consumer World's What's New
http://www.directory.net/dir/whats-new.html (Click on: "How
to submit listings").

What's New Too
http://newtoo.manifest.com/WhatsNewToo/submit.html
This site promises to post your listing within 36 hours.

A Directory of 500 online malls:

http://nsns.com/MouseTracks/HallofMalls.html

Links to over 200 Web directories, Search engines and link services

Go Net Wide   http://www.GoNetWide.com/gopublic.html

GLOSSARY

anonymous FTP site
An FTP site that can be accessed by anyone.

Archie
An Internet feature used for searching files that are located on anonymous FTP sites.

ASCII
American Standard Code for Information Interchange. A system that assigns numeric codes for every letter of the alphabet (and punctuation marks). By using this system, any computer on the Internet can communicate with other computers (at least at the level of simple text messages).

analog line
A simple telephone line that requires digital data to be converted to analog data in order to be transmitted through it.

auto responder
An e-mail feature that sends an e-mail message to anyone who sends it a blank message (or a message with certain key words). It uses a program called *mailbot*, and its function is not unlike that of a fax-on-demand.

backbone networks
Central networks with high speed computers to which all the other networks of the Internet are connected. Most are maintained by the National Science Foundation.

BBS

Bulletin Board System. A server computer that is connected to the Internet through a modem. It can offer the same services as a Web site, but it is not an integral part of the Internet.

bps

Bits per second. A unit of transmission speed (of electronic data).

browser

A software (e.g., Netscape) that allows Internet users to view World Wide Web sites.

chat programs

Discussion forums that allow users to communicate with each other in real time (unlike e-mail). They can be either text or voice based.

client

Any computer that connects to another computer in order to retrieve data from it, or to use its software. A program can also be considered a client. For instance, Mosaic (a type of browser) is a Web client: it utilizes Web features and displays Web information on the user's screen.

cross posting

Posting one message to several newsgroups.

cyberspace

Although this term has no exact meaning, it is usually applied to the online world or its digital traffic.

dial up account

The basic Internet connection that allows individual users to log onto the Internet through a modem.

digital line
A high speed line that can transfer digital data without the need to convert it to analog data first. Such lines (e.g., T3, T1) are much more expensive than the regular analog lines, but they allow for much higher transmission speeds.

domain name
A combination of letters or numbers that leads to the online address of a computer or a network. The domain name's structure varies according to the Internet feature the addressee is using (Web, gopher), the type of organization (commercial, government) and the addressee's country.

download
To copy a file from a remote location (e.g., a server) to the user's computer.

E-cash
Electronic cash. A currency that can be exchanged over the Internet. The user is required to purchase the electronic currency from a special bank. He or she can then use it to purchase goods from Internet vendors who accept E-cash.

e-mail
Electronic mail. This feature allows Internet users to send and receive messages online.

FAQ
Frequently Asked Questions.

firewall
A security feature that protects networks or computers from unauthorized access by Internet users. Only if you intend to

connect directly to the Internet should this concern you (server services usually take care of this for you).

flame
The e-mail equivalent of hate mail. Tens and even hundreds of such hate messages can be sent to the victim's e-mail box at a time. Internet users might do this to businesses that send them unsolicited e-mail.

freeware
Any software that is distributed free of charge for unlimited use (also see: **shareware**).

FTP
File Transfer Protocol. This is a feature that enables the transfer of files (not just ASCII text files) over the Internet.

Gopher
An Internet feature that arranges files under a system of hierarchical directories. It presents users with a clear menu that allows them to search information and even browse through other Gopher sites. **Gogherspace** is the collective name for all these sites.

hit
A recorded visit (of an Internet user) to a site. If a Web site records 200 hits, it means that it was visited 200 times (but not necessarily by 200 different users).

home page
In any Web site, this page functions as the gate. The site's menu is displayed there, plus any general information about the company or the site.

host
Any computer that allows another computer to retrieve information or access its files.

HTML
HyperText Markup Language. A system of commands that allows a file (text, graphics) to function as a Web page. It allows files other than ASCII to be viewed by Web browsers.

hypertext
When HTML properties are assigned to plain text, it becomes hypertext. Clicking on **hypertext** will link the user to a different place on the Web page, to a different Web page, or to a different site altogether.

Internet
A collection of about 20,000 networks that connect to several backbone networks.

IP
Internet Protocol. A system of sending and receiving information as a series of independent packets. Naturally, this protocol must be used by any computer that is connected to the Internet.

ISDN
Integrated Service Digital Network. Digital lines that can transfer data at speeds of 64,000 bps and up.

LAN
Local Area Network. Any computer network located within the same building or complex. They usually do not have to rely on telecommunication equipment for connection between the LAN's components.

link
A connection between two sites. For example, clicking on a hypertext that reads <u>White House</u> can take the user to the White House's Web site.

LISTSERVE
An e-mail program that creates and runs mailing lists.

mailbot
See: **auto responder**

mailing list (online)
A list of e-mail addresses of people who are interested in receiving messages from a certain source (or from each other). For example, a mailing list set up by a movie fan to let people know of new developments in the movie industry.

Meta file
A file attached to an HTML document that includes data such as title, author, description, and keywords. Such files can be read by search engines.

MLM
Multi Level Marketing. Also known as network marketing. See details in page 173.

modem
A device that converts digital information to analog information (and vice versa) in order to enable such information to be sent over ordinary telephone lines.

Network marketing   See **MLM**

newsgroups
(a.k.a. USENET newsgroups) A forum that is used by

Internet users to post their messages and form discussion groups dedicated to a variety of subjects.

online
Any computer that is connected to another computer is "online."

online mall (or virtual mall)
A collection of virtual stores under one menu or directory. Sometimes the mall acts as the online businesses' server service, and at other times it only provides links to their sites (as well as advertising space).

online world
A collective term for all computer networks, whether or not they are a part of the Internet.

packet switching
The breaking down of digital information into several packets that travel independently to their destination and reconstruct the complete message once they arrive there. This technology forms the basis of the Internet.

POP
Post Office Protocol. This protocol allows Internet users access to their e-mail boxes (which are located on their e-mail server's computers).

press release
A report (on a new site, business, product, book) sent to newspapers and magazines for the purpose of being published by them.

protocol
A set of rules by which computers communicate with one another.

search engine
An online database that allows Internet users to locate and reach Internet sites.

server   See: **host**

server service
A business that connects directly to the Internet and that rents out space on its computers. By doing so it allows individuals and businesses without a direct connection to the Internet to set up a presence (e.g., a Web site) there.

service provider
The connection between the individual and the Internet. The subscriber is connected to the service provider through a modem, and the service provider connects to the Internet through other networks (such as the backbone networks). The subscriber can view Internet sites, but his only online presence is usually an e-mail box.

shareware
Any software that is purchased on approval. The customer downloads it for a predetermined trial period, and must pay the creator if he wants to use it beyond that period.

site
A collection of files (text, graphics) that exists online under one domain name.

spamming
Posting an unsolicited commercial message to newsgroups, sending such a message to private e-mail boxes, or otherwise using unethical promotional tactics online.

UNIX
The Internet's operating system. Unix is to the Internet what DOS is to PCs.

upload
To copy a file from the user's computer to a remote location (usually a server).

URL
Universal Resource Locator. An addressing system used for finding Web sites.

USENET newsgroups   See: **newsgroups**

user (often: Internet user)
A person who logs onto the Internet.

virtual
A common definition of anything that exists only in cyberspace (or in other words: something that has no physical existence): a virtual store, a virtual mall.

virtual Web server
A site that is connected to the Internet through another server in a way that creates the impression that it is connected directly to the Internet.

WAN
Wide Area Network. A network that is spread over a large area, even across several different countries. Telecommunication equipment is required to connect the WAN components.

Web
See: **World Wide Web**

Web master
A person in charge of maintaining a Web site; a new job definition in today's corporate America.

World Wide Web (a.k.a. "the Web" or "WWW")
An Internet feature that allows users to view (or download) any file: text, graphics, video, audio, software. It understands various commands that can be given by clicking on an icon or text (see: hypertext).

zine
Online Magazine.

INDEX